For my partner, Anne, without whose
help, support and encouragement
this book would not exist.

EAGLES HIGH was devised and produced by
Wordwright Books
2 – 6 Ellington Place
Ellington Road
London N10 3DG

Designed by: **Peter North**

Editorial Team: **Judith Hayter** (Editor),
Dennis Knight, Simon Parry
Production Co-ordinator: **Erica Rosen**
Production (Imago): **Lorraine Baird,
Penny Cooper, Michelle Morton,
Kate Walker**

Researchers: **Wing Commander
N P W Hancock, DFC, RAF** (Ret'd),
Dennis Knight, Simon Parry

Photograph by courtesy of Air Chief
Marshal Sir Christopher Foxley-Norris,
GCB, DSO, OBE, RAF (Ret'd)

First pubished in Great Britain in 1990 by
Leo Cooper Limited
190 Shaftesbury Avenue
London WC2H 8JL

Typeset by: **Helen Robertson, London**
Page make-up by: **Terry Heighington,
Mike Heighington Design Ltd, London**
Originated by: **Bright Arts, Hong Kong**
Printed and bound in Italy by: **Imago
Publishing Limited**

ISBN 0 85052 889 5

Eagles High

Peter North

LEO COOPER · LONDON

Foreword

'The Battle of France is over ... the Battle of Britain is about to begin. The whole fury and might of the enemy must soon be turned on us. Hitler knows that he will have to break us in this island or lose the war ... let us therefore brace ourselves to our duties, and so bear ourselves that, if the Empire and its Commonwealth last for a thousand years, men will say, 'This was their finest hour.' WINSTON CHURCHILL, 1 JULY 1940

The 50th Anniversary of the Battle of Britain is generating a spate of literary material. It is perhaps surprising that there remains enough of interest to write about a subject which has been so exhaustively covered in both fact and fiction.

To encounter a book, then, that at this late date treats an old theme in a fresh and original way is a rewarding experience. *EAGLES HIGH* is unlike any other book I have read on the subject. Peter North's artwork is outstanding in its originality, accuracy, and beauty. The text too has been checked and cross-checked to a high standard of accuracy. One is pleased to note, for example, that it pays fitting tribute to that fine officer, Sir Hugh Dowding, and — as a former Hurricane pilot — that it puts into proper perspective that doughty aircraft's contribution to the Battle. Already too many myths have grown up around the Battle of Britain. To illustrate the point, if one asked the mythical man on the Clapham omnibus who won the Battle of Britain, he would probably answer: 'A handful of dashing young officers flying Spitfires.' If he did, he would be wrong on three counts at least.

The 'handful', the legendary Few, in fact numbered nearly 3,000, that is to say the number of aircrew who actually fought in Fighter Command during the official period of the Battle, 10 July – 31 October, 1940 (this timescale itself seems somewhat questionable and arbitrarily selected — there was plenty of hard fighting before 10 July and after 31 October). Note that I write 'aircrew', not 'pilots'. Ten per cent of today's veterans of the Battle of Britain Fighter Association are Observers and Air Gunners, who flew in Blenheim fighters or the ill-fated Defiants. But of those who did so fight, only a few, a small proportion averaging perhaps 600 to 700, were in front-line squadrons at any one time. The rest were under re-training, or instructing, or recuperating from extreme operational exhaustion, burned, or wounded, or otherwise *hors de combat*.

But of course it was not only the aircrew who won the Battle. Without the backing of the technical ground crews and airfield services; of the men and women in the maintenance and support systems, in the Ground and Control network and the Radar stations, in the whole administrative and domestic systems of the airfields, the efforts of the aircrew would have been in vain and short-lived. They were gallantly supported also by the other RAF Commands — Bomber, Coastal and Training; by the Navy (2 Fleet Air Arm Squadron fought the Battle as well as a number of individuals); and by

the Army, notably Anti-Aircraft Command. Nor should we ever forget the spirit of the British people, who were the first to stand up to the weight of German bombing. *EAGLES HIGH*, I am happy to report, pays fitting tribute to all these too often unsung heroes of the Battle.

'Dashing young officers'? The backbone of the Fighter Squadrons in 1940 were the regular NCOs. Sergeant Pilots like Lacey, Wilkinson and Hallowes, who constituted one third of the squadrons' strengths, and often far more of their skills and experience. Nor was 'young' always appropriate. Men like Bader and Malan were in their thirties at the onset of the Battle and many of their Polish and Czech comrades older yet. It was their maturity and experience that provided the essential leadership for the younger and more excitable pilots.

'Spitfires'? The facts are that twice as many Hurricanes participated as Spitfires, and their pilots scored twice as many victories.

Happily, Peter North repeats none of these fallacies. In fact, *EAGLES HIGH* is one of those rare books that helps dispel the myths that obscure the truths of those times. It is a book worthy of its subject matter — and a most fitting 50th Anniversary tribute.

Air Chief Marshal Sir Christopher Foxley-Norris, GCB, DSO, OBE, RAF Ret'd, Chairman, Battle of Britain Fighter Association

The Battle of Britain

The twentieth century will forever stand out in the annals of military history as the century that saw warfare take to the skies. And if there is one air battle that epitomizes all the courage and craziness, all the skill, romance and sheer hard work of the aerial pioneers, it is without doubt the Battle of Britain.

The Few. The finest hour. Already the phrases ring with the mellow tones of myth. Indeed, to those of us who were not numbered among the Few, they are figures of superhuman stature, heroes in a world of puny players. But they were made of flesh and blood like us, and their achievements are all the more remarkable for that. Before the mists of time swirl them out of reach, we should reclaim their feats from the mythmongers and celebrate their achievements for what they are: the work of real men — young men, sons and brothers and boyfriends — fighting to master their machines and instruments, as well as their nerves, sweating and toiling on the ground as in the air.

The battle involved not just men but women, many of whom were WAAF plotters. The RAF pilots and groundcrew came from many nations — Britons, Canadians, New Zealanders, Australians, South Africans and Americans as well as airmen from countries overrun by the Germans. These included Poles, Czechs, Belgians and Frenchmen. All these were flying and servicing the fighter aircraft — those fragile, vulnerable, graceful, death-dealing machines in which the aerial combatants fought their duels throughout the summer and autumn of 1940.

Heroes need worthy opponents, however. The Few would not have achieved their legendary status otherwise. Without the brave and skilful Luftwaffe pilots, there would have been no battle over Britain.

Thus, any honest account of the Battle of Britain must encompass more than the heroics and aerobatics that marked out this significant year of the Second World War. We need to understand why the battle ever came about, who exactly the combatants were, and what their leaders meant to achieve by this series of spectacular clashes. We ought to examine this newly evolving war machine, the armed aircraft — after all, it was less than forty years since the Wright brothers had achieved the first ever powered aeroplane flight: it was, in other words, a shorter span of time since man had first flown than has elapsed between then and now.

We must pay credit where it is due: to the aircraft designers and builders, to the veteran fighter pilots from the First World War and to those who kept aviation alive during the inter-war years. But most of all,

it is fitting that we honour the memory of those few hundred young men — many of whom did not survive — who held back the Nazi tide in 1940, when the evil spawned by Adolf Hitler threatened to spill across the English Channel.

The Seeds of War

By the end of June 1940, Britain stood alone against the Nazi tide. Most of Europe lay prostrate beneath the fascist jackboot. Hitler's empire stretched from Scandinavia to the Mediterranean, from the Atlantic to the Balkans, and his war machine was now poised to invade Britain. But why? Why had the German people rallied to the Nazi cause? Why did those young men and their aircraft ever have to clash in the skies over Britain?

Ironically, the answers lie in the conclusion to the earlier war — the Great War, the 'war to end all wars', the First World War — which had ended in undeniable defeat for Germany. The mere fact of defeat was bad enough for a nation that held military prowess in such high regard; but the deliberate humiliation wreaked by the victors upon the vanquished acted like a spur to their numbed or inert self-esteem. It was the sheer unremitting bitterness of humiliation that provided such fertile ground for the deadly harvest of Nazism.

The armistice signed on 11 November 1918, in the converted restaurant car of a railway train in the forest of Compiègne, in northern France, was followed by a treaty of settlement signed at the Paris Peace Conference on 28 June 1919. This Treaty of Versailles, as it became known, was the repository of all the justifiable anger of the conquering nations — and of their less praiseworthy desire for revenge and recompense.

After four grim years of carnage, especially in the trenches of western Europe, the victorious allies felt no cause for magnanimity: France, in particular, insisted that Germany be made to pay for her sins. In addition to territorial losses, Germany had to submit to allied troops occupying the Rhineland and the Saar; had to make financial reparation of millions of pounds; had to sign a clause confessing her guilt in causing the war; and had to watch her once proud war machine being dismantled — her army demobilized and guns melted down, her battle fleet surrendered to be divided among the victors, her air force disbanded and aircraft confiscated.

It was too much. The military blamed each other and the politicians who had let them down. Forcibly disarmed, they huddled in conspiratorial indignant groups, discussing the mistakes of the past and searching for a new strategy. The courageous and successful airmen, who had fought to the last, saw their beloved aeroplanes commandeered while they themselves were grounded, forbidden even to go near an aircraft: a cruel fate for men impelled by their passion for flying. But it was the German navy that made the grand gesture.

On 21 June 1919, in Scapa Flow, the Orkney Islands anchorage of their erstwhile enemy's Home Fleet, the German naval commanders scuttled their ships rather than swallow their pride. At a signal from Admiral von Reuter, and under the very noses of the British, silently the eleven battleships, five battle-cruisers, eight cruisers and thirty-six destroyers sank beneath the cold dark waters.

It was a tragic loss of a fine battle fleet, which profited only the family of scrap merchants who were still salvaging the fleet when the Second World War broke out. It was also an act of defiance, affording a certain grim satisfaction for the moment at least.

Angry and bewildered, the German people watched their homeland collapsing in political and economic chaos. The terms of the Treaty of Versailles left them seemingly impotent in the face of a hostile world. But there were some who found loopholes in the treaty, and who realized that the new international watchdog, the League of Nations (created at the same Paris Peace Conference), was toothless. Although conceived in good faith the League was doomed to failure from the very start when several world powers, including the United States and Russia, refused to join. At its peak there were sixty member nations, but they could only recommend political measures and economic sanctions. They had no power to use military action. The treaty might ban the military machine, but industrial production would be stepped up. An air force might be forbidden but technical expertise could still be honed in the service of civil manufactures, or temporarily exported to the benefit of less advanced nations such as Russia. Armed defiance was out of the question, but semi-clandestine gatherings of like-minded men seeking a new framework for the future could not be prevented. Thus, while a half-crazed corporal found an outlet for his prejudices with the embryo Nazi party, his future *Reichsmarschall*, Hermann Göring — former commander of the famed Richthofen squadron — was disconsolately seeking a living as an aircraft salesman in Sweden.

In Britain, meanwhile, with the euphoria of victory worn off and unemployment stalking the land fit for heroes, the only thoughts cast in Germany's direction were prompted by continuing resentment. As the politician Sir Eric Geddes had proclaimed in an election speech in December 1918, the Germans had to be squeezed 'until the pips squeak'. The seeds of the next war were already being sown.

While the victors of the First World War squabbled over the spoils to be exacted from the vanquished, the interned German fleet lay at anchor in Scapa Flow. The skeleton crews aboard the wallowing, idle ships had plenty of time to nurse their grievances and plan revenge. Bitterly digesting the news that their fleet would be split up and shared among the victors, on 21 June 1919, at a prearranged signal from their Admiral, the German commanders scuttled their warships — worth an estimated £70 million.

Terms of Malice

At the end of the First World War, the winning nations (principally Britain, France and the USA) met in Paris to discuss what damages should be paid by Germany and her colleagues in defeat (Austria, Hungary, Turkey and Bulgaria). The Treaty of Versailles, signed on 28 June 1919, embodied the terms of settlement to be imposed on Germany — a settlement so vindictive that it directly contributed to the resentment on which Hitler built his Nazi Reich.

The leading players at the Paris Peace Conference were Lloyd George, the British Prime Minister; Clemenceau, the French premier; and Woodrow Wilson, President of the USA. The latter had created a fourteen-point peace plan, on the basis of which Germany had sought an armistice. But Wilson's idealistic notions were no match for the sceptical Europeans; the caustic Clemenceau, in particular, so offended him that America refused to ratify the Treaty.

Like Lloyd George, Clemenceau was a pragmatist, but was pressured by the French military into imposing the harshest possible terms. His British counterpart was urged into sterner measures by his fellow MPs. Indeed, the populations of both France and Britain were baying for vengeance. And so the two leaders agreed to the unrealistic terms of the Treaty of Versailles.

The German army would be cut to 100,000 men with no tanks, no aircraft and no heavy artillery.

All German colonies were to be surrendered.

The region of Alsace-Lorraine was to be returned to France, and other German borders redrawn to the benefit of Belgium, Poland and the new state of Czechoslovakia.

The coal-rich area of the Saar was to be run by France, under the eye of the newborn League of Nations, while the mineral-rich Rhineland would submit to Allied occupation for fifteen years and then be permanently demilitarized.

Germany was to pay financial reparations, fixed in 1921 at £6,600 million.

Germany should sign a clause in the Treaty admitting liability for the war.

The economic terms of the Treaty were criticized even at the time for being unenforceable. With Germany's industrial heartlands under foreign control, there was no way she could meet the financial reparations. In fact the German people were literally dying of starvation, and had to be supported with huge loans from America and Britain.

By 1923 Germany had defaulted on her reparation payments, and France and Belgium invaded the Ruhr valley to recuperate their losses. The German leaders responded by deliberately creating hyperinflation that reduced debts — but also savings — to negligible proportions. By 1929, in the worldwide recession following the Wall Street Crash, the embittered German people were ripe for the totalitarian stability offered by Hitler's Nazi Party.

Lessons Lost

The development of the aeroplane has been so swift that it is easy to forget the first flight was piloted by Orville Wright barely one lifetime ago, on 7 December 1903. For a moment in history, mankind paused to marvel at this new toy — yet only nine years later the toy had become a weapon: aircraft were used, albeit ineffectually, to deliver bombs during a minor colonial skirmish in North Africa between Italy and Turkey. And, by the start of the First World War, the aeroplane's potential was clear to all but the wilfully blinkered.

Initially the aeroplane was seen primarily as a mobile observation platform, an improvement on the kite balloon: the pilot could swoop over enemy lines to report on troop movements, or call down artillery fire with previously unattainable accuracy. Gradually, however, he came to play a more active role, using pistol, rifle and machine gun to increasingly lethal effect, as with ever more sophisticated equipment he sought to wrest control of the skies from his enemy counterpart. This is how thousands of brave men met their death: shot in the sky or trapped in a damaged machine plunging to the earth.

Such aerial duelling is an integral part of any picture of air combat in the First World War, but it is not the whole picture. By 1918, the fighter pilot's attention was already being divided between enemy fighters and bombers. For the menace of bomber aircraft was beginning to dawn on civilian populations, as air raids grew in number and in effectiveness, their targets including not only military installations and aerodromes but also railway lines and major highways. And public concern quickly focused authority's attention on the need for fighter aircraft as a front-line aerial defence.

Whether bombers or fighters, the German airmen, before they even took off, had the advantage of good organization behind them, whereas the muddled chain of command for the British included the Royal Navy Air Service, Royal Flying Corps, Air Board, Ministry of Munitions, Admiralty and War Office. The British also laboured under the handicap of obsolescent aircraft, outclassed in speed, manoeuvrability and armament. As a consequence

of taking the fight into enemy territory, British casualties in early 1917 rose from 56 in January to 117 on a single day in April — and this at a time when recruitment and training of pilots was already conducted with almost indecent haste.

It was in 1917, however, that the British single-seat fighter or 'scout' — the Sopwith Pup, for instance — began to gain the upper hand. The courage and inventive tactics of the few hundred British airmen, raising an aerial barrier that even the most aggressive of German raiders found it hard to penetrate, gradually earned them control of English skies: a supremacy later extended to key areas of continental Europe. Now there was time to digest those hard-won lessons: to consider why certain tactics, some machines, individual men, were more successful than others.

Obviously speed was important to a fighter aircraft, along with a reliable engine and fuel system. Less obviously, and paradoxically, handling was best if the machine was unstable; that is, if it responded to the pilot's every demand, right or wrong, without trying to regain level flight. The successful fighter

The 1916 Royal Aircraft Factory RE.8 (nicknamed 'Harry Tate' after a music hall comedian), with a top speed of 100mph (161kph), was only 20mph faster than the BE.2 it replaced, and to the war's end was easy meat for any German fighter.

In 1916, Anton Fokker developed a device that allowed a machine gun to fire through the arc of a propeller without shooting it off. His one-gun Eindekker E.I was so feared that in its short era it was known as 'the Fokker scourge'.

aircraft had to be manoeuvrable on all axes, light on the controls and should not yaw or pitch even when the gun was fired, had good all-round vision and — preferably — offered the pilot some protection against enemy sharpshooters.

The successful fighter pilot was generally young, with fast reactions, both physical and mental. He was so confident of his machine and his mastery of it that he could dive, roll, fly without regard to the horizon and still shoot straight when in the mêlée of a dogfight. Another vital skill he acquired was 'fighter pilot's eye': the ability to focus on infinity in an empty sky, in order to spot the distant speck of an approaching aircraft. Two further qualities were not capable of being taught but could certainly be encouraged: the 'killer instinct' or will to win, a ferocious competitive streak that did not admit even the possibility of defeat; and luck. Only with lavish helpings of luck did a man survive to become an ace.

As for tactics, they were best conveyed in the deliberately clichéd phrases designed to lodge in a man's mind. Beware of the Hun in the sun. Always

Spring 1918:
jousting above the trenches, the RFC's 138mph (220kph) SE.5A had a 20mph advantage over the Albatros DVs of von Richthofen's 'flying circus' (the black one flown by Göring).

The 1916 Vickers FB.5 Gunbus, a two-seat fighter with a forward-firing single gun and a 'pusher' propeller, had a top speed of just 70mph (113kph) and could seldom catch a German aircraft.

try and fight with the advantage of height. Get in close and fire short bursts. It's the one you don't see that gets you. Don't fly straight for more than three seconds in combat. And that perennial favourite: discretion is the better part of valour.

These were the lessons lost: lessons learnt the hard way by men with unique personal experience of combat, who could have passed on their knowledge if only it had been recognized as valuable. But in Britain after the First World War, those who held positions of power were often from the old guard, unable to comprehend this new dimension of warfare. The very same lessons would have to be learnt all over again by the next generation of fighter pilots.

The Best Flying Club in the World

Fortunately for Britain, there were a few individuals who saw not only the future potential of air power but also the present need to capitalize on what had so far been learnt: men such as General Hugh Montague Trenchard, who had commanded the Royal Flying Corps during the First World War.

Trenchard, later appointed Marshal of the RAF and honoured with a viscountcy, is justifiably regarded as the father of the Royal Air Force. It was he who presided over the amalgamation of the RFC and Royal Naval Air Service in 1918 and who fought to establish an air force worthy of the name. By the end of 1919 he had drawn up a detailed plan for the development of the RAF, and this plan, with very few alterations, became the basis of Britain's future air power. But it was many years before the country's political leaders allowed Trenchard's ideas to be implemented in full — by which time he himself would be lost to the RAF. Indeed, the RAF itself almost ceased to exist following cuts which reduced personnel from 291,000 in November 1918 to just 78,300 in March 1920. By a strange quirk of fate it was saved from extinction only when it was seen to have played an important role in the Turko-Greek war and in Egypt.

The nation's dominant concerns now were social and economic. The war had been won and Germany had been tamed by the Treaty of Versailles, so why should anyone waste time and money planning for another war? A 'ten-year rule' was imposed, which effectively decreed that air force requirements could be shelved for the next decade. Inevitably the RAF was demobilized, reduced to one tenth of its wartime strength; experienced veterans returned to civilian life or, at best, to life behind a desk where it was all too easy to forget the realities of war.

'The destruction of nations will be accomplished … by aerial forces,' wrote the Italian Giulio Douhet in 1921, and the primary threat was the bomber aircraft; more controversially, he argued that the best defence against this threat was — likewise — the bomber aircraft. His views were shared by the British air chief. Always offensively minded and acknowledging the high cost of defensive fighter patrols, Trenchard believed, like most of his contemporaries, that civilian populations would be so terrified of bombing raids that they would pressurize their leaders into surrender. He thus favoured an air force that comprised two bomber squadrons to every fighter squadron.

The new air force was small, select, drawn from the educated classes. Trenchard was aiming for quality; but this was too often interpreted as privilege. The young men recruited from public schools to train as pilots were used to the gentlemanly life, and at the new officer cadet colleges they found it: servants to bring them morning tea and press their gaudy uniforms, and plenty of leisure for sport and partying. Their flying skills were learnt in fragile, exhilarating, open biplanes, going solo after the first eight to ten hours of instruction, then pursuing a year's studies — meteorology, navigation, radio technique — while practising the new skills and learning more. They were then assessed for more advanced training and, according to temperament and predilection, assigned to either bomber or fighter squadrons.

Now the young pilots were intended to widen their experience of both aircraft and tactics. Formation flying was designed to enable commanders without radios to control large teams. Carefully choreographed manoeuvres were meant to simulate attacks on what was usually a single, slow, unrealistic target. Year by year, the training grew less relevant to modern requirements and the aircraft more outdated. Trenchard's scheme was not at fault; nor were the spirited young men. What was needed was government recognition — and finance.

In 1929 Trenchard left the air service. He had watched over its birth and set it on its feet, fought for its very existence and guided it through a time of severe economic restraint; he could do no more.

The nation itself, seemingly content to regard the RAF as a group of travelling entertainers, gathered in enthusiastic crowds to gasp at spectacular aerobatic displays. The young pilots honed their useless skills and yearned for a posting to the Middle East, where they could bomb rebellious musket-wielding tribesmen.

The only jarring note came from the war veterans,

who scathingly dismissed the RAF as 'the best flying club in the world'. But as they watched these ritualized flying displays the memories of air combat came flooding back, and they shuddered in apprehension for the moment when these young men met reality.

Spreading Wings

It was not just the RAF, of course, that laid on exciting stunts to entertain the public. All over the world, demobilized airmen who had acquired the taste for flying sought by any means to continue. Throughout Europe and North America, groups of pilots tried to earn a living with their barnstorming, joy rides and flying circuses. Amongst them were some far-sighted aviators who, having made contact with men of means, jointly began to plan their vision of the future: speedy mail delivery, and faster, safer, more comfortable passenger services.

Flying displays were all very well; they attracted attention and converted a handful of intrepid joy-riders to the cause of aviation. But flying was about to become big business, and it was not just the far-sighted few who saw the need for more sophisticated aircraft in the future, as well as improved navigation and air traffic control.

Scott and Campbell-Black make a dawn take-off from Mildenhall in their DH.88 Comet 'Grosvenor House' to win the 1934 MacRobertson race to Melbourne, closely followed by KLM's DC.2.

While more and more old aircraft were taking to the skies, bought from decommissioned air forces along with unwanted airfields, the race was on to build better and faster aeroplanes. And, while the finance-starved RAF was making do and mending, civilian entrepreneurs were already operating the world's first regular airlines. By 1919 there was a scheduled passenger service between London and Paris, and in 1924 five small British airlines merged to form Imperial Airways which was soon opening up air routes not only to Europe but to the Middle East (1927) and India (1929).

Thus it was mainly the civilian enthusiasts and commercial entrepreneurs who prompted the development of modern aircraft.

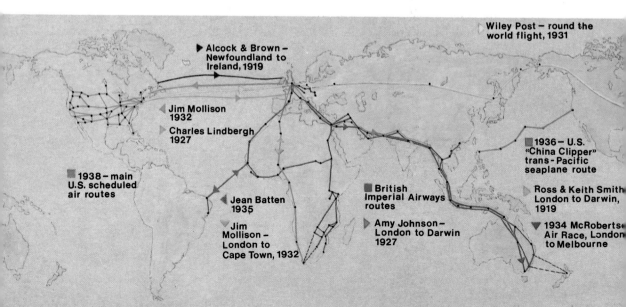

Wiley Post – round the world flight, 1931

▶ Alcock & Brown – Newfoundland to Ireland, 1919

▶ Jim Mollison 1932

▶ Charles Lindbergh 1927

■ 1938 – main U.S. scheduled air routes

▶ Jean Batten 1935

▶ Jim Mollison – London to Cape Town, 1932

■ British Imperial Airways routes

▶ Amy Johnson – London to Darwin 1927

■ 1936 – U.S. "China Clipper" trans-Pacific seaplane route

Ross & Keith Smith London to Darwin, 1919

▼ 1934 McRoberts Air Race, London to Melbourne

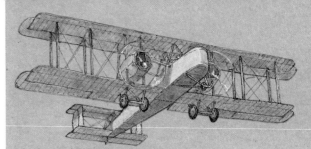

Partly to win public kudos and partly to encourage this private enterprise, air-minded governments joined news-seeking Press proprietors and other wealthy individuals in offering large prizes for flying achievements. One constant challenge was the Atlantic: despite Alcock and Brown's pioneering flight in 1919, many lives were lost in pursuit of Atlantic records, even after the first non-stop solo flight in 1927, in a specially built monoplane, by Charles Lindbergh.

Designers, manufacturers and pilots, eager to stretch their wings and prove their supremacy in this competitive new world, were only too keen to take the bait. Even women joined in. Records were broken with increasing regularity. In 1919 it took Keith and Ross Smith, with mechanics Shiers and Bennett, thirty days to fly to Australia; in 1930 Amy Johnson made it in just nineteen days. In 1931, Wiley Post's 'Winnie Mae' took him round the world in less than nine days. The world was shrinking fast, and the aircraft was taking on a sleek new shape. In the 1934 MacRobertson Air Race, from England to Australia, the first of the twenty aircraft to reach Melbourne safely was the specially built DH.88 Comet racer, which had averaged a speed of 177mph (285kph) over the distance of 11,300 miles (18,182km); but the race was won on handicap by an elegant all-metal DC.2 airliner entered by KLM (Royal Dutch Airlines), forerunner of the Second World War's ubiquitous DC.3 Dakota.

The monoplane was by now established as the design of the future. While giant, sedate old biplanes carried passengers in Pullman-like luxury, with restaurant, lounge and sleeping cabins, and graceful flying boats swooped down on rivers or delivered rich tourists from one lakeside hotel to another, the mail and more time-pressed passengers were increasingly carried in the faster, more efficient, metal monoplanes. Most of the world's major cities were now linked by scheduled air routes, and the network was expanding with phenomenal speed.

The private enthusiasts and commercial pioneers had demonstrated the abilities and limitations of the aeroplane, had stretched it beyond endurance and yet survived to tell the designer where changes were needed. Thanks to them, many an air force observer learnt, at second hand, important lessons of airmanship, as well as the value of engine design, fuel type, streamlining and strength. Safety, paramount for passenger aircraft, was of interest to the military too; the lives of those expensively trained young pilots were too valuable to be wasted in accidents resulting from an engine fault, for example.

It was, in short, thanks to private aviation that the British government was eventually persuaded to sanction the RAF's efforts to modernize its aircraft, and ultimately, in 1934, to approve the Air Ministry's specifications F.36/34 and F.37/34, the fruits of which would be the Spitfire and the Hurricane.

Above: Vickers Vimy Bomber, flown from Newfoundland to Ireland by Alcock and Brown and from London to Darwin by the Smith brothers in 1919. Power: Two 360hp Rolls-Royce Eagle VII engines. Wingspan: 67′ 2″ (20.47m). Length: 43′ 6″ (13.26m). Weight: 12,500lb (5675kg). Top speed: 103mph (166kph). Standard range: 985 miles (1585km).

Above: 'Jason', the DH60G Gipsy Moth used by 22-year-old Amy Johnson on her 19-day solo flight from Croydon to Darwin, Australia, in 1930. Engine: 120hp DH Gipsy 4. Span: 30′ (9.1m). Length: 23′ 11″ (7.3m). Weight: 1400lb (636kg). Top speed: 105mph (168kph). Range: 320 miles (512km).

Below: 'Winnie Mae', the Lockheed Vega 5.B flown round the world in 1931 by Wiley Post and Harold Gatty — 15,474 miles (24,903km) in 8 days, 15 hours, and by Post solo in 1933 in 7 days, 19 hours. Engine: 420hp Pratt & Whitney Wasp. Span: 41′ 0″ (12.50m). Length: 26′ 6″ (8.08m). Weight: 4750lb (2157kg). Speed: 220mph (354kph).

Below: 'Nordmeer', one of three 4×604hp Junkers Jumo diesel-engined Blohm und Voss Ha.139 floatplanes operating the first transatlantic mail service from 1937, using a catapult depot ship to refuel off the Azores.

Schneider Trophy

The single greatest impetus to aircraft development before the Second World War was supplied by just one man, Jacques Schneider. Born into a wealthy munitions family in France in 1887, Schneider grew up with a taste for adventure, speed and danger; balloons, racing cars, aeroplanes attracted him in turn — but in 1912, the injuries he received in a motor-racing crash forced him to give up flying. However, reluctant to turn his back entirely on the thrills of aviation, he decided to institute an annual

Below: Although they never met in real life, the 440mph (703kph) Macchi 67 is shown flying over the Supermarine S.6B, the outright winner of the Schneider Trophy in 1931.

seaplane race, the winner to receive a large bronze and marble trophy.

The first Schneider Trophy races were held before the First World War. The rules were very strict: competitors had to take off from and land on water, and had to follow a tight triangular course. France won in 1913, with a Deperdussin monoplane; in 1914 Britain won with a Sopwith Tabloid biplane. The opposition was negligible, and the competition more notable for farce than technical progress: half the seaplanes crashed while the others could not even get into the air. The competition was halted between 1914 and 1918 due to the Great War, but the war proved to be an even greater spur for aircraft development.

The race was reinstated after 1918 but still the

spectators came to chuckle rather than applaud. In 1919, one aircraft nearly sank when it hit an obstruction in the water, but the young designer — R. J. Mitchell — was not deterred; he knew his Supermarine Sea Lion had potential.

By 1923, the Schneider Trophy had gained considerable prestige in aviation circles, and the rivalry between national teams, backed by government money, had taken on a serious edge. In that same year, the team from the United States of America won with a streamlined float biplane which reached a speed of 177mph (285kph). In 1925 the Americans again trounced the opposition, principally Britain and Italy, with an improved Curtiss biplane that won at a speed of 232mph (373kph). Confident of their superiority, the

Americans then relaxed — and as a result lost the trophy to Italy in 1926, when an 800hp Macchi monoplane achieved 246.5mph (396kph).

Reginald Mitchell, by now chief designer for the Supermarine company, had learnt the same lesson: that a monoplane would invariably beat even the most streamlined of biplanes. Over the next five years the Schneider Trophy, by now a biennial contest, was a thrilling duel between the British Supermarines and the Italian Macchi seaplanes. In 1927 Britain took first and second places with Supermarine S.5s, powered by 875hp Napier Lion engines. In 1929 Britain won the trophy again, with Supermarine S.6s now powered by Rolls-Royce engines. If the British team won for a third time in succession, according to the rules of the competition the Schneider Trophy would be theirs to keep.

At this precise moment, the British government withdrew financial backing. Despite intense lobbying from the Air Ministry, the vital subsidy was denied to the Supermarine company. It looked as if the 1931 race would be won by the Italians by default. Only when a wealthy private benefactor stepped forward, Lady Houston, with a donation of £100,000, could the British team proceed.

The Italians, meanwhile, had been furiously developing their engines, with all their hopes pinned on the superb Macchi 67; at the last minute it let them down and they were obliged to withdraw. The French entrant crashed. The 1931 race was therefore won by a Supermarine S.6B, with a 1900hp Rolls-Royce engine, which cruised round the course at a speed of 340mph (547kph) — the Schneider Trophy had been won outright. (It is now in the Royal Aero Club, London.)

The race machines were pedigree hand-built freaks. The engines, for example, had to be rebuilt after only an hour's running. They were designed specifically to meet the challenge of the Schneider Trophy: that is, the challenge of speed. On the surface, it may seem that this dangerous series of seaplane races had no more relevance to military reality than the formation-flying display teams touring the country in their biplanes. In fact, however, the leading aviation designers of the day had pointed the way to the future. Design, materials, engine power and fuel, aerodynamics, handling: everything was pushed to the limit in pursuit of the Schneider Trophy, and with national honour at stake the participating governments were forced to take a close interest.

Now, as the 1930s again raised the spectre of war — first in the Far East, where Japan was threatening British interests, then much closer to home where the German war machine was tuning up — Britain was relying on private investment to fund the development of her aircraft industry. Only at the eleventh hour, and thanks to the efforts of a few strong-willed individuals, was Britain able to meet the menace currently embodied in one man: Adolf Hitler.

Above: The Sopwith Tabloid in which Howard Pixton won the race in 1914 at an average speed of 87mph (140kph). It was a seaplane conversion of a landplane designed by Tommy Sopwith, later famed for his WW1 Camel fighter.

Above: After the war, national pride became a factor in the Trophy races. The Americans used this Curtiss biplane to win the event in 1925 at an average speed of 232mph (373kph), flown by Army pilot Billy Mitchell, later to be court-martialled for sinking a battleship in a bombing demonstration.

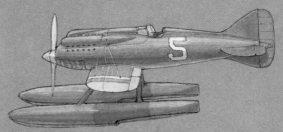

Above: Italy, the only other country to take the Trophy seriously, won in 1926 with this Macchi M.39, powered by an 800hp Fiat engine and flown by Major de Bernardi, at an average speed of 246mph (396kph).

Below: The Supermarine S.5, which in 1927 won the first of a hat-trick of victories and thus helped to win the Trophy outright for Britain. Powered by a Napier Lion engine and flown by an RAF pilot, Fl. Off. S. N. Webster, it achieved an average speed of 282mph (453kph). The designer, R. J. Mitchell, made good use of his experience with these fast seaplanes when he created his famous fighter, the Spitfire.

Rise of the Third Reich

When the First World War ended, Corporal Adolf Hitler was in hospital, temporarily blinded by a British gas attack in Flanders. He was thirty years old, twice decorated, and unable to accept the fact of defeat. Austrian born, he had joined a Bavarian regiment and identified with the German 'master race', dreaming of greatness; now his dreams were shattered, his country's future bleak. Yet in less than sixteen years, he would be Führer of the Third Reich.

It was his sheer refusal to face facts that helped Hitler through those dark times. Focusing on his belief that Teutonic people were the true masters of the world, that all other nations were inferior and that Jews in particular were responsible for all his country's woes, he joined one of the workers' parties springing up in 1919 and found his voice in public harangues. Quick to express the widespread anger and bitterness over the punitive terms of the Treaty of Versailles; equally quick to note the political vacuum as the Weimar Republic stumbled from crisis to crisis, Hitler displayed remarkable acumen as he led his National Socialist German Workers' Party through the years of chaos. The country wanted a strong leader; he would be that leader. The people wanted to believe in Germany's greatness; he would give them greatness.

The rhetoric, promises and romantic notions of Wagnerian grandeur found a ready audience in the disillusioned German population. Mass unemployment and hunger had aggravated the humiliation of defeat; people listened to this strangely charismatic speaker and digested his words eagerly. Many of them shared his anti-Semitism, feared the Communists, despised the gypsies and homosexuals. No matter that he had adopted the fascist paraphernalia then associated with the Italian leader Mussolini: the military values, marches, swastika crosses and raised-arm salute. Hitler's skilful propaganda was balm to the ordinary German.

In November 1923 Hitler thought his moment had come. Launching the 'Munich putsch', as it later became known, he attempted to seize control of the Bavarian government — and for his presumption was thrown into jail. But his sentence, as well as the sixteen Nazi 'martyrs' who had died during the putsch, only served to enhance his reputation. Moreover, he made good use of his thirteen-month imprisonment, dictating *Mein Kampf* ('My Struggle') to an apostolic fellow prisoner. Upon his release he was lionized by politicians and industrialists who thought they could manipulate him and use his popular support for their own ends. But Hitler turned the tables on them; by promising economic stability and future strength in return for their backing, he welded them into his iron plan for Germany.

The failure of the Munich putsch was a setback for the four German fascist groups, but elsewhere fledgeling right-wing extremist parties were growing in popularity. During the mid-1920s the German fascist movement was silenced by increasing national prosperity and an acceptance by other nations of the German Republic, but in other countries fascism was gaining hold. Benito Mussolini led the Italian fascists into power in Italy in 1922; he even gained sufficient support from industry and the armed forces to be appointed Prime Minister by King Victor Emmanuel. In 1923 a fascist régime was established in Spain and this was followed in 1926 by similar régimes in Poland and Lithuania.

The opportunity the German fascist parties needed, however, was suddenly thrust upon them. In October 1929 the Wall Street crash signalled the beginning of a worldwide economic depression. In the 1928 elections, the year before the crash, the Nazi party won a handful of parliamentary seats. In 1930, the year after, they won 107; and two years later they more than doubled *that* figure. In January 1933 Hitler was proclaimed Chancellor — and within months he had imposed his totalitarian régime.

The 'Third Reich' had begun.

Undoubtedly, by spending public money on rearmament and on grandiose civic projects, Hitler managed to reduce unemployment. The economy, after the worldwide ravages of the Depression, was under control. But the price Germany paid for this stability was extreme. Democracy was dead. In 1934 Hitler was proclaimed Führer of the Reich, head of state as well as commander-in-chief of the armed forces. Now his brown-shirted paramilitary thugs came into their own, not only terrorizing his opponents, but strutting through the cities to attend rallies addressed by the Führer and leading the reconstituted German army in pursuit of his expansionist plans. Elitist groups of secret police and security forces such as the SA, SD and SS were formed. At the end of June 1934, Hitler ordered his SS troops to assassinate the head of the SA, Ernst Rohm. Following the death of President von Hindenburg, in August 1934, Hitler moved quickly to expand Germany's military might and made public the existence of the Luftwaffe in March 1935. Later that same month conscription into the military forces was reintroduced. In September 1935, the Nuremberg Laws initiated the long period of victimisation of German Jewry with legislation specifically discriminating against Jews. In 1936, in direct contravention of the Versailles treaty, Hitler sent German troops into the Rhineland.

It seemed as if Hitler's promises were to be fulfilled. Germany was prosperous, united, recovering her self-esteem. The Third Reich would grow, expand, take in Austria and Czechoslovakia. All Europe would acknowledge German supremacy. It would be the 'Thousand-Year Reich'...

From Defeat to Defiance

11 November 1918. Germany admits defeat by signing the armistice marking the official end of the First World War.

28 June 1919. In the Treaty of Versailles the victorious powers attempt to wreak revenge on Germany. Their demands for financial reparation, however, are so excessive as to be unenforceable and ultimately counter-productive.

31 July 1919. The constitution of the Weimar Republic guarantees a federal democracy under President Ebert (succeeded in 1925 by von Hindenburg). The aftermath of the war creates enormous economic difficulties for the new German leaders; the nation suffers financial collapse in 1922–23.

8 November 1923. Hitler launches the 'Munich putsch', which, although it ends with him in jail, succeeds in making him known to the German people. Above all, he wins support for his rejection of the Versailles Treaty.

30 January 1933. The Nazis having won a majority in the German assembly, President von Hindenburg appoints Hitler as Chancellor.

27 February 1933. The Reichstag, housing the German parliament, is destroyed in a fire which Hitler blames on the communists: he uses the incident as an excuse to suppress all opposition.

23 March 1933. Hitler suspends the Weimar Republic, creating what is in effect a one-party state. The 'Third Reich' is born.

2 August 1934. Von Hindenburg dies and Hitler is created 'Führer' and Supreme Commander of the Reich. For the next year he concentrates on rearmament and economic expansion.

9 March 1935. The existence of the Luftwaffe is announced to the world, and one week later conscription is introduced.

7 March 1936. The demilitarized zone of the Rhineland is reoccupied by German troops, in direct contravention of the Treaty of Versailles — eliciting international protest but no retaliation.

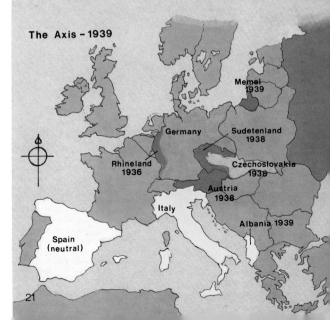

The Axis – 1939

Memel 1939

Germany

Sudetenland 1938

Rhineland 1936

Czechoslovakia 1938

Austria 1938

Italy

Albania 1939

Spain (neutral)

The Eagles Soar

Young Germans, using a technique employing an elastic pull-rope, launch a potential Luftwaffe pilot on his path to the Battle of Britain from an Austrian hillside in 1933.

Hitler's rapid rise to power was duplicated, despite the Treaty of Versailles, by the rise of the military. Under the terms of the treaty, Germany was allowed to maintain a small militia of 100,000 men. The navy and air force were, as we have seen, disarmed and disallowed. But if the German military leaders were initially cast down by their defeat, a growing indignation and scorn for the treaty led them to evade its restrictions in both letter and spirit.

Chief architect of the early rebirth of German military power was General Hans von Seeckt, head of the Reichswehr from 1919 to 1926. Although himself an army man, he foresaw the value of a strong air force, and managed to include in the Reichswehr not only his most experienced infantry officers but also 180 former air force officers — including men of the calibre of Kesselring, Sperrle and Stumpff whose Luftflotten 2, 3 and 5 would confront the RAF during the Battle of Britain. Thus, while men like Göring were disbarred from flying in their own country, a useful nucleus of senior airmen was growing in Berlin.

Even more important, thanks to von Seeckt there was soon to be a stock of young, eager pilots — trained in, of all places, Russia.

In 1921 von Seeckt struck a secret deal with Communist Russia. The Soviets wanted to borrow German expertise; the Germans wanted merely somewhere to practise their forbidden military activities. As a result, by 1924 the Germans had three secret bases in Russia; one, at Lipetsk, southeast of Moscow, was to be the birthplace of the Luftwaffe.

Supplied by Anton Fokker, scourge of the RFC, the aeroplanes at Lipetsk were fitted with specially imported British Napier Lion engines.

This irony was compounded by the fact that during the 1920s, at the very time when Britain's aircraft industry was in decline due to RAF cutbacks, German aviation was expanding. The dithering Disarmament Commission seemed incapable of deciding whether the defeated nation's civil air industry should be permitted. Manufacturers like Junkers, Dornier and Heinkel quietly returned from abroad and resumed production, turning out metal monoplanes ostensibly for sport; if sport specifications were exceeded, the aircraft were secretly shipped to Lipetsk. Sports flying and gliding were permitted under the terms of the treaty and the association of flying clubs, the Luftsportverband, was remarkably popular with young men of military age and bent.

In 1926 Germany's Lufthansa airline was allowed to operate in open rivalry with Britain's Imperial Airways, and under the astute commercial direction of its chairman, Erhard Milch, the future field marshal, Lufthansa's networks expanded far and wide. In addition, the airline became a training ground for many more future Luftwaffe airmen. Moreover, Milch soon found a powerful supporter in the Nazi ranks: Hermann Göring.

Göring had returned from Sweden and, throwing in his lot with Hitler, was one of those injured during the Munich putsch. Now a rising Nazi politician, he was elected to the Reichstag in 1928. Von Seeckt had been ousted, the victim of hierarchical wrangling within the Reichswehr, but his legacy to Germany was the military framework on which Hitler and Göring would build. In fact, it was initially Milch who devised the resurgence of the nation's air power; his two Nazi patrons, busy with politics, were content to leave it in his hands. Using Lufthansa as a cover, he encouraged the development and production of new aircraft designs; the training of aircrews; the specialized instruction at Lipetsk. He monitored the technical developments on show in the Schneider Trophy races and at other international flying meets, and fostered the military potential of supposedly commercial aircraft. But Milch's very success led to his downfall; eventually Göring saw him as a rival and had him demoted.

In 1935 Germany went public, announcing to the world that she had created her own modern air force, the Luftwaffe. The world, still suffering from post-Depression blues, paid scant attention. When the Luftwaffe's commander-in-chief boasted that this was the strongest air force in the world, his claim was dismissed as preposterous. As yet the international community knew nothing of the secret military programme behind Lufthansa, still less of the young 'eagles' fresh out of the Russian nest. But uneasy suspicions were deepening almost by the day.

Young Luftwaffe pilots, trained to fly Ju.52 *(left)* and FW200 airliners in 1937, would soon be flying them as Luftwaffe transports and patrol aircraft after the war started.

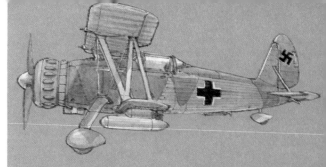

Above: The Arado Ar.197 was the last biplane fighter designed in Germany. Of all-metal construction, it was intended for use on the proposed aircraft carrier *Graf Zeppelin* which was never completed. It first flew in 1937, but the project was shelved later that year, after just three prototypes had been built.

Below: In 1934 the German airline Lufthansa commissioned designs from the Dornier aircraft construction company for a fast new mail-carrier with capacity for six passengers. Three prototypes were evaluated but rejected on the grounds that passengers would have serious trouble boarding them. At this point the project was very nearly scrapped. It was rescued by Robert Untucht from the German Air Ministry, who thought it would make a good bomber. A fourth prototype was built, with its cabin portholes filled in and a new twin-fin tail: the Do.17 bomber was born.

Below: By contrast with the Do.17, the Ju.87 was always intended to be a warplane. The German Air Ministry issued specifications for a *Stuka* (dive-bomber) in 1934, and the Junkers prototype — powered by a British Kestrel engine — took to the air in 1935. Early design faults were soon ironed out, and the two-man bomber demonstrated its accuracy with devastating effect in Spain and Poland. It fell easy prey, however, to the fast British fighters.

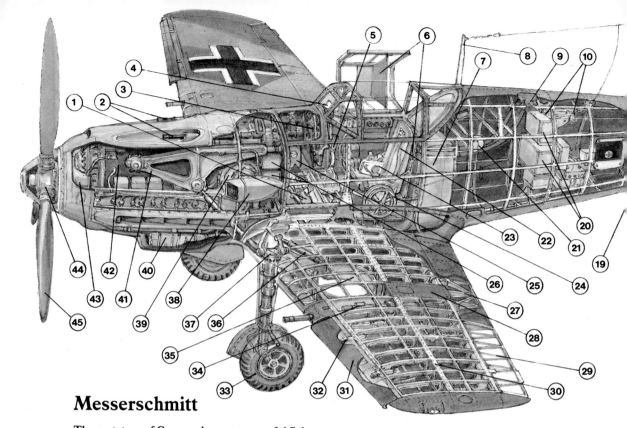

Messerschmitt

The prototype of Germany's most successful fighter plane first flew in September 1935: ironically with a British engine, a 695hp Rolls-Royce Kestrel, as its own engine was not ready. Designed by Willi Messerschmitt at the Bayerische Flugzeugwerke (Bavarian Aircraft Works) in Augsburg, the Bf.109 — not until 1944 was it officially renamed Me.109 — was one of four rival manufacturers' machines built to Luftwaffe specifications and competing for the prize of an air force contract. Despire fierce personal animosity between Messerschmitt and Milch, the Bf.109 won the prize. Within months it was in production, taking multiple shape on the assembly lines.

An advanced, all-metal monoplane, Messerschmitt's single-seat fighter was based on his successful four-seater Bf.108 *(see opposite)*, built in 1934; but, from the very beginning, the 109's deficiencies were plain and it underwent considerable modification. The square, overloaded wings, despite automatic leading-edge slats, could cause a vicious stall on banking too tightly. The widely splayed undercarriage was prone to collapse on landing. On take-off, the aircraft had a tendency to swing. Poor visibility resulting from the long nose and hefty bracing on the cockpit canopy led to many a minor accident on the ground. Much more seriously, its fuel capacity — and thus its range — was limited.

Nevertheless, the Bf.109, particularly in its later versions, tested and proved in the Spanish Civil War, was a fast, powerful and well-armed fighter which, for all its faults, earned an enduring place in history.

Key:

1. Rudder pedal. 2. 2×7.9mm MG.17 machine guns. 3. Instrument panel. 4. Reflector gunsight. 5. Control panel. 6. Armour plate behind pilot. 7. Fuel tank (88gal/400l). 8. Radio aerial. 9. Fuel filler cap. 10. Radio tray supports. 11. Tailplane incidence jack. 12. Rudder. 13. Rudder trim tab. 14. Elevator. 15. Tail main spar. 16. Tailplane brace. 17. Tailwheel shock absorber. 18. Tailwheel. 19. Battery. 20. RT radio. 21. Oxygen cylinder. 22. Bucket seat and safety straps. 23. Throttle and mixture controls. 24. Tail trim and undercarriage emergency handwheels. 25. Oil reservoirs. 26. Ammunition boxes. 27. Flaps. 28. Cannon ammunition

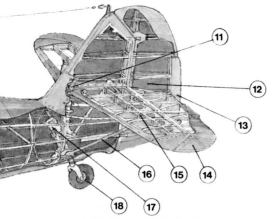

Bf.108 Taifun 1934

Designed for sport or light transport, the Bf.108 was an immediate success. The flush-rivetted, stressed-skin construction gave it strength for aerobatics. Wing flaps and slats eased low-speed handling and permitted a stalling speed of 53mph (85kph), while a 230hp Renault or 270hp Argus engine gave a top speed of more than 190mph (305kph). Its spirited and tractable performance made it an ideal trainer for the Bf.109 fighters reaching service in 1937.

From the flight of the prototype in 1935, the Bf.109 was continually uprated. The 109C-1 model, powered by a 730hp inverted V.12 Junkers Jumo 210Ga and constant-speed propeller, weighed 5062lb (2298kg) when loaded and carried four 7.9mm machine guns at a top speed of 292mph (470kph). Span: 32′ 4″ (9.87m). Length: 28′ 0″ (8.55m). Ceiling: 27,560ft (8400m). Time to 16,400ft (5000m): 8.75 min. Max. range: 404 miles (650km).

access panel. 29. Aileron. 30. Main wing spar. 31. Leading-edge wing slat. 32. Slat slide track. 33. Main wheel. 34. Port 20mm MG.FF cannon. 35. Undercarriage well. 36. Undercarriage retraction actuating piston. 37. Undercarriage pivot. 38. Carburettor air intake. 39. Supercharger. 40. Glycol cooling radiator. 41. Engine bearer. 42. Daimler Benz DB 601A engine. 43. Glycol header tank. 44. Constant pitch gearbox. 45. Three-bladed metal propeller.

Bf.109E-4 Specification

Wingspan: 32′ 4″ (9.87m). Length: 28′ 8″ (8.74m). Gross weight: 5053lb (2294kg). Engine: 1150hp Daimler Benz 601A. Armament: 2×7.9mm machine guns with 1000 rounds per gun and 2×20mm cannon with 60 rounds per gun. Top speed: 354mph (570kph). Ceiling: 36,089ft (11,000m). Range: 410 miles at cruising speed. Rate of climb: 3000ft/min (914m/min).

Bf.109E-4 Cockpit

1. Reinforced windscreen. 2. Revi mirror-reflector gunsight. 3. Blind-flying panel, including altimeter, magnetic compass, direction indicator, ASI, bank and turn indicator, artificial horizon, and rate of rise and descent indicator. 4. Flare pistol. 5. Control column handgrip with gun-firing button. 6. Engine and fuel state instruments, including low fuel warning light. 7. Throttle and mixture lever quadrant. 8. Rudder bar pedal. 9. Elevator trim and emergency undercarriage lowering handwheels. 10. Pilot's bucket seat to take parachute, with straps.

Bf.109C-1 1938

Bf.110 — *Zerstörer*

While the Bf.109 was being developed and gearing up to full production, Messerschmitt started a new project: a fast, twin-engined, long-range heavy fighter which would accompany the bombers and destroy (*zerstören*) any hostile fighters. The Bf.110C-4 (*below*) was powered by two 1100hp Daimler Benz 601A engines, carried a crew of two over 530 miles (853km) and was armed with four 7.9mm MG.17 machine guns and two 20mm MG.FF cannon firing forward with one MG.15 machine gun for rear defence. With a top speed of 249mph (400kph) at 23,000ft (7000m) and a ceiling of 32,800ft (10,000m) it seemed a formidable opponent. Aircrews assigned to Bf.110 units were considered an élite force, and the aircraft's initial performance did indeed augur well. But when the Bf.110 encountered the RAF single-seat fighters, its faults were immediately

clear. It was too heavy and unwieldy; for all its weight of fire-power, it was no match for the nippy Hurricanes and Spitfires. By September 1940, Bf.110 bomber escorts had themselves to be escorted by single-seat Bf.109s. The *Zerstörer*, as Göring called it, never lived up to expectations.

Hurricane

Although outshone by the legendary Spitfire in terms of grace and speed, the Hurricane was the RAF's front-line aircraft in the Battle of Britain. A sturdy, reliable, effective fighter, the 'Hurry' is still remembered with affection by those who flew it.

The Hurricane acquired its name in 1936, some three years after Sidney Camm, chief designer for the Hawker Aircraft Company, began discussing a monoplane successor to his biplane Fury. Camm, awarded a knighthood in 1953 in recognition of his services to aviation, at first envisaged his 'Fury Monoplane' as a purely private venture; the RAF was still reliant on his biplane and considered monoplanes too new and risky. But with Hitler now in power and Germany known to be rearming, in 1934 the growing international tension prompted the issue of two new Air Ministry specifications for what would become the Hurricane and the Spitfire.

Camm's monoplane had already spent many long months on the drawing board, and his design was now quick to take off. The prototype first flew in November 1935, by which time its original Goshawk engine had been swopped for the PV.12, another Rolls-Royce engine better known as the Merlin. Despite being bigger and heavier, the Merlin added over 100mph to the Hurricane's speed.

The early version's traditional fabric-covered metal frame, with wooden formers, gave it great strength. The thick wing not only produced a rate of climb higher than almost any aircraft of its time, but could also house eight .303″ (7.70mm) machine guns, each with 500 rounds of ammunition, all firing outside the propeller arc. The retractable undercarriage was robust enough to withstand repeated bumping on grass airfields, and — due to the wide, split, trailing-edge flaps — landing speeds were little more than 57mph.

In the air, although slightly heavy, the prototype Hurricane proved to have excellent flying qualities: positive to handle, with a tight turning radius and providing a stable gun platform. So confident were they of its potential that, even before the official order came in, Hawker set their assembly line in motion and the first production model took to the skies in October 1937. But it was not until May 1938 that the Hurricane attracted public attention, when Flight Lieutenant John Gillan flew from Edinburgh to London in less than an hour — albeit with the aid of a tailwind.

Refinements made to the Hurricane by the spring of 1940 included the fitting of a three-blade, constant-speed propeller; an armour-plated bulkhead and bullet-proof windscreen; and metal-skinned wings (though the fuselage retained its fabric covering), which increased weight but improved overall performance. Although slower by 30mph (48kph) than the Bf.109, the Hurricane proved itself a match for the German fighter. Indeed, two thirds of all enemy aircraft — both fighters and bombers — shot down during the Battle of Britain could testify to the excellence of the Hurricane.

A 1940 Hawker Hurricane, Mark I

1. Rotol constant-speed propeller gear. 2. 1030hp Merlin II V.12 engine. 3. Engine bearers. 4. Carburettor supercharger air inlet. 5. Undercarriage retraction ram. 6. Rudder bar. 7. Main-spar wing attachment point. 8. Gun bay with 500-round ammunition storage boxes. 9. .303″ (7.70mm) Browning machine guns. 10. Landing light. 11. Flaps. 12. Engine oil radiator. 13. Main fuel tank (33gal/150l). 14. Retractable stirrup step. 15. ½″ (12.7mm) steel plate. 16. Rat-trap hand hold. 17. Fixed castering tailwheel. 18. Elevator. 19. Rudder trim tab. 20. Tail light. 21. Rudder. 22. Rudder post. 23. Elevator trim tab. 24. Airframe framework. 25. Radio aerial. 26. VHF/RT radio. 27. Flare chutes. 28. Pilot's bucket seat and harness anchorage. 29. Sliding cockpit cover. 30. Throttle and mixture lever. 31. Rear-view mirror. 32. Control column, with gun trigger button on hand ring. 33. Reflector gunsight with adjustment for range and brightness. 34. Instrument panel. 35. Reserve fuel tank (28gal/127l). 36. Fire wall. 37. Header tank for glycol ethylene engine coolant. 38. Aileron in starboard outer wing. 39. Starboard navigation light. 40. Rotol 3-bladed wooden propeller.

Hawker Fury, No. 1 Squadron, RAF, 1934

This single-seater biplane was used by the RAF's fighter force until supplanted by the Gloster Gladiator in 1937. Engine: 525hp Rolls-Royce Kestrel. Top speed: 207mph (313kph). Span: 30′ 0″ (9.144mm). Length: 26′ 8″ (8.13m). Armament: 2×.303″ (7.70mm) Vickers machine guns. Service ceiling: 29,500ft (8,992m).

Hurricane prototype, 1935

K5083 first flew on 6 November 1935, surpassing all but its designer's specifications. Fitted with the new Merlin engine, retractable landing gear and eight Browning machine guns, in February 1936 it underwent formal RAF trials; although it performed superbly, flying at 315mph (476kph) in level flight and climbing to 15,000ft (4615m) in six minutes, it was three months before the Air Ministry's official order was received.

Private Venture

Despite their success in the sporting and commercial worlds, the Air Ministry persisted in the belief that monoplanes were unsound. This would have been disastrous but for the initiative of commercial manufacturers and private individuals. In 1935, for example, the Bristol Aeroplane Company built a twin-engined bomber: but the Ministry refused to fund its development. Only a donation from Lord Rothermere, the Press baron, allowed the project to continue. Then, seeing the Bristol Blenheim outperforming all comparable aircraft, the Ministry was forced to place an official order.

Spitfire

It was a 'bloody silly name' for an aircraft, in the opinion of R. J. Mitchell, but what did he know? He was merely the designer of this most elegant and effective of fighters.

In fact 'Spitfire' had been the unofficial nickname for Mitchell's earlier design, the 1931 Type 224, which was his response to an Air Ministry specification for a new fighter. His company, Supermarine (later a division of Vickers), specialized in seaplanes; as we know, a Supermarine S.6B won the Schneider Trophy in 1931. However, Mitchell realized that all-metal monoplanes would lead the way into the future, and persuaded Supermarine to enter his design for the RAF trials even though the Ministry wanted a biplane. But Type 224 was outclassed by the Gloster Gladiator, and he returned to the drawing board.

Mitchell's new design, Type 300, was revolutionary. The elliptical wing, though thin, was deep enough to house the specified eight guns and the outward-retracting undercarriage. The slim fuselage and traditional wooden propeller belied its powerful Rolls-Royce PV.12 engine, the Merlin — the same engine that powered the Hurricane.

Spitfire IIa

1. Rudder trim tab. 2. Rudder post. 3. Tailwheel shock absorber. 4. Elevator. 5. Flare chutes. 6. RT radio. 7. Aerial. 8. Oxygen cylinder. 9. Control column. 10. Mirror. 11. Reflector gunsight. 12. Upper fuel tank. 13. Fuel filler cap. 14. Engine bearers. 15. Merlin engine. 16. Undercarriage well. 17. Gun access panels. 18. ASI pitot tube under wing. 19. DH constant-speed gear and propeller. 20. Glycol header tank. 21. Trolley-ac. plug. 22. Main spar. 23. Undercarriage pivot. 24. Main wheel down. 25. Broken gun patches. 26. Fabric-covered

Despite the long nose which restricted vision, Type 300 was a joy to fly. It first took to the air in March 1936, four months after the prototype Hurricane, and proved an immediate success.

Mitchell had watched Hitler's rise to power with the growing conviction that war was inevitable, and struggled to complete modifications to his masterpieces. Sadly, he never saw it in its finest hour; he died of cancer on 11 June 1937, at the age of just forty-two. At least by then his graceful Spitfire was already in production, on the way to stardom not just in aviation annals but in the popular imagination.

ailerons. 27. Rear spar. 28. Four starboard Browning .303 machine guns. 29. Compressed air breech-cocking piston. 30. Wing rib over wheel well.
31. Glycol cooling radiator (oil cooler under port wing).
32. Split flap. 33. Compressed air reservoir. 34. Lowered bucket seat. 35. Half-inch armour plate. 36. Fuselage stringer. 37. Former. 38. Flush-rivetted stressed dural skin. 39. Castering tailwheel. 40. Elevator main spar.

Cockpit (below): 1 rear-view mirror.
2 Bullet-proof (toughened glass) windscreen. 3 Mirror-reflector gunsight, with adjustable range markers.
4 Engine and fuel gauges. 5 Blind-flying instrument panel (clockwise): ASI, artificial horizon, rate of climb, bank and turn, direction indicator and altimeter.
6 Gun-firing button on control column hand ring. 7 Throttle and fuel mixture lever quadrant. 8 Rudder pedals. 9 Elevator trim tab adjustment wheel. 10 Pilot's parachute forms cushion in bucket seat, which can be raised to allow better view for take-off and landing if canopy is open.

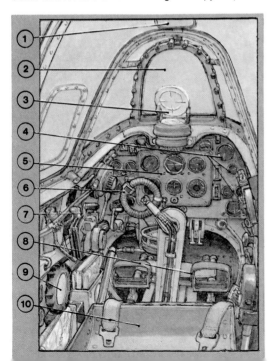

Supermarine Type 224 — 1934

The 224 was built to meet the Air Ministry specification for a four-gun replacement for the 174mph (280kph) Bristol Bulldog biplane fighter. It was not a success. The engine was a 650hp Rolls-Royce Goshawk, with a complicated evaporation cooling system that constantly failed. Although the all-metal construction and open cockpit echoed the best racing machines of the day, the 224's top speed of 238mph (383kph) and its rate of climb did not match that of its chief rivals

Supermarine Type 300 — 1936 Spitfire prototype

K5054, the Spitfire prototype, first flew from Supermarine's Eastleigh airfield on 6 March 1936. It featured stressed-skin monocoque construction, closed cockpit, retractable undercarriage and flaps to reduce take-off and stalling speeds. Like the Hurricane, it was powered by a Merlin engine, the 990hp Merlin C, which enabled speeds of up to 348mph (560kph). It was armed with four (later eight) Browning .303 machine guns. For grace and pleasure in handling, this aircraft was unique.

Spitfire IA — 1940

The first production order, for 310 Mark Is, reached Supermarine in July 1936: a huge order for this small company, which therefore had to sub-contract most of the work. By the spring of 1940 nearly 1500 had been ordered, but only about 250 delivered.

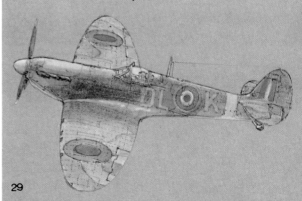

Nationalist
advances on
the North

Santander

Nationalist held
territory at the
end of August,
1936

Madrid

Nationalist advance
on Madrid,
July/August,
1936

Portugal

Seville

Granada

Morocco

and fighters. The Russians countered by supplying I.15 Chato biplanes, flown by their own volunteers for the Republicans. These were outclassed by the Heinkel He.51s, which themselves were no match for the I.16 Rata monoplanes, which in turn were eventually overcome by the new Bf.109s. The Messerschmitts confirmed their superiority with a decisive victory at Brunete in July 1937.

The irony of two nations that had shared training facilities at Lipetsk now fighting at arm's length in Spain was not yet appreciated by the rest of the world. So traumatized by the last war and its bewildering wake of social uncertainty, still smarting from the Depression and nervous about revolutionary Russia, many people preferred to ignore the conflict in Spain. Some, like Sir Oswald Mosley, the British MP who had flown with the RFC, and Charles Lindbergh, the American aviation hero, openly embraced fascism. Others, though censorious of Hitler, saw communism as the greater threat and surreptitiously encouraged the rise of any régime that could act as a buffer between Russia and the west.

Only the cold-blooded German bombing raid on Guernica provoked a real international outcry, and by then it was too late. The young eagles of the Condor Legion, led by men like Adolf Galland and Werner Mölders, had acquired invaluable experience of combat and rehearsed tactics that would soon prove so useful elsewhere — like the new, open, two-plane formation, the *Rotte*, which could be doubled up to a four-plane *Schwarme*, allowing each pilot to watch his companions as well as the sky around him (the RAF, adopting the same technique, called it 'Finger Four').

When the Spanish finally laid down arms, the Nationalists having taken Madrid at the end of March 1939, the foreigners retired well satisfied — particularly the Germans. Hitler's tanks and aircraft, and the men behind them, were ready. While Spain now licked her wounds, the rest of Europe was about to erupt.

A Heinkel He.51
biplane being
attacked by
I.16 Ratas.

Dress Rehearsal

The first spasm of war to seize Europe was in Spain. While the world's attention was focused on Hitler's rampant rearmament in Germany, in Spain the socialist Republicans were in power. But not for long. In July 1936, General Franco led the military rebellion that resulted in the Civil War and his own thirty-six-year dictatorship. And, while Spaniard fought Spaniard, their country became a testing ground for modern weaponry and tactics — including aircraft.

Right from the start, it was German aircraft that gave Franco the edge. Over a period of three months, Junkers Ju.52 trimotor transports, clandestinely sold to the insurgent army, ferried 20,000 Spanish troops from Morocco to southern Spain. This, the first great air lift in history, enabled Franco to establish an Army of the South which later linked up with General Mola's Army of the North and thus cemented a solid base from which to attack. Further aid came from Mussolini's Italy, including more than 700 aircraft.

The Republicans, ill-organized and squabbling among themselves, had lost control of half of Spain before they recovered from their shock and sought foreign aid. Russia supplied over 1000 aircraft; another 500 or so arrived from sympathizers in other countries.

By November 1936 Germany had set up the so-called Condor Legion in Seville, commanded by General von Sperrle and comprising both bombers

France

Catalonia
River
Ebro

Barcelona

Madrid

Final Nationalist
campaigns for
Madrid and
Catalonia in
1938/1939 and
Nationalist territory
in February 1939

A Messerschmitt Bf.109B being assembled for the Condor Legion.

The Spanish Civil War

At the start of the 1930s, Spain was a country of deep divisions: a monarchy buttressed by the Catholic Church and armed forces, but with a poverty-stricken, backward agricultural base, and a political class weakened by ideological dissent.

In April 1931, King Alfonso XIII, identified with the right-wing dictator Primo de Rivera, fled the country in the face of growing Republican sentiments. The Republicans gained an uncertain ascendancy, marred by communist and anti-clerical atrocities, which in 1933 provoked Primo de Rivera's son, José Antonio, to found the Spanish fascist party: the Falange. Similarly resentful of socialist unrest, elements of the armed forces conspired to overthrow the legitimate government, taking as their champion Francisco Franco, the cautious clever military governor of the Canary Islands.

Hitler and Mussolini both saw the conflict in Spain as an opportunity to test modern armaments and practise new skills; Stalin contributed military aid; but the rest of the world turned its back on Spain. Apart from the idealists who fought in the International Brigades, most of the foreign combatants were 'volunteers' sent by Hitler, Mussolini and Stalin. The rest of the international community followed a policy of non-intervention, formalized in London in September 1936, though more honoured in the breach than the observance.

On 1 October 1936 Franco was proclaimed Generalissimo and head of state of Nationalist Spain. With the Falange (though José Antonio was shot in November), he established a one-party government modelled on the Italian system. The Republicans, however, rallied by the Catalans and Basques, retained control in the east and north. When Franco tried to break through the Republican line and advance on Valencia, at the end of

1937, he was repulsed; but after a year-long battle of attrition the Nationalists, aided by increased matériel from Germany and Italy, finally took Catalonia in early 1939 and gradually mopped up the remaining resistance.

This was the reality of civil war, aided and abetted by outsiders. While cynical foreigners were engrossed in the comparative performance of aircraft, tanks, bombs and techniques, Spanish families were riven by tragedy and loss — which soon would be shared by families the world over.

A Bf.109 shooting down an I.16.

Blitzkrieg

In September 1938, even as the Spanish war continued, Hitler was threatening to invade Czechoslovakia, where the German-speaking minority in the industrialized province of Sudetenland was agitating for union with Germany. At last the world began to wake up. Hasty measures were effected to mobilize armies or emphasize neutrality, according to bent; to turn industry's production lines over to military purpose; to prepare uncomprehending but fearful civilian populations for the totality of modern war. Yet still, at this eleventh hour, the world's appeasers cheered when the British Prime Minister, Neville Chamberlain, returned from Munich with his sheet of paper promises and his talk of 'peace for our time … peace with honour'.

At this time Hitler was going out of his way to entertain many of the world's leaders at his newly constructed 'Eagle's Nest' in the Alps. Chamberlain was among those given a warm welcome and photographed with his congenial host. But behind the friendly façade worked an evil mind.

Honour was just an empty word to Hitler; all he understood was force. Relishing the clear superiority his Luftwaffe and tanks had demonstrated in Spain, and thwarted in his attempt to flaunt it in Czechoslovakia, he now sought a new parade ground — and found it in Poland.

Stalin, angered by the Munich agreement to divide Czechoslovakia, which he saw as western imperialism spreading eastwards, signed a secret pact with Hitler: in effect, they agreed to split Poland between them. On 1 September 1939, Germany invaded Poland. It was a well co-ordinated land–air attack, later to become familiar as the Blitzkrieg ('lightning-war') technique. The Luftwaffe led the way, the bombers destroying communications and airfields while bands of Messerschmitt Bf.109s and 110s fought off any Polish aircraft not destroyed on the ground. The panzer (armoured) forces, including motorized infantry, made a rapid advance on several fronts at once, seizing bridges, railways, any key positions, but always thrusting forward.

Within a fortnight half of Poland had fallen. Warsaw was surrounded, though resisting bravely.

Then came the last blow: Russia attacked from the east. Ten days later the whole country lay under Nazi–Soviet domination.

Heartened by the news that Britain and France had declared war on Germany, the Poles had fought back fiercely and inflicted heavy casualties on the invaders. But the Blitzkrieg had taken them by surprise. The German bombers — Heinkel 111s, Dornier 17s and 215s, Junkers 88s — had wrought havoc on civilian as well as military targets. Wherever resistance threatened to delay the panzer troops they radioed for air support, usually Junkers 87s, the precision dive-bombers known as 'Stukas' (*Sturzkampfflugzeug*: literally 'dive-attack aircraft'). This new single-engined two-man bomber, first tried out in Spain, was fitted with a

Polish campaign, September 1939

Wehrmacht infantry and Panzer tanks shelter as Luftwaffe Ju.87 Stuka dive-bombers deal with a pocket of resistance hindering their advance into Poland in September, 1939.

siren which screamed as it fell out of the sky in a near-vertical dive, a terrifying sound to anyone below. The Bf.109 had proved its supremacy, and the 110 'Destroyer' had justified its name by inflicting dire punishment on ground targets.

Overall, Hitler was well satisfied with progress in Poland. The Blitzkrieg technique could be relied upon to produce results. The Luftwaffe had delivered. The panzer army had got through. The Poles had retaliated with unexpected vigour but they had been beaten. So what if the British and French had declared war on Germany? They had done nothing about it yet. And, when he was ready, he would launch another Blitzkrieg on them.

Go East

Hitler had resurrected the nineteenth-century German concept of *Lebensraum* (literally 'living space') as an excuse to pursue his megalomaniacal dream. That living space would be found in the east, where the racially inferior peoples of Czechoslovakia, Poland and the Ukraine would serve the needs of the master race. Or such was his reasoning.

After the *Anschluss*, the union with Austria in March 1938, and then the ceding of Sudetenland to Germany in September, Britain and France had hoped that Hitler's territorial ambitions would be satisfied. In vain. In March 1939 Germany seized the Czech provinces of Bohemia and Moravia — and still the Western Allies did nothing. The sacrifice of Czechoslovakia had not prevented war, merely delayed its onset.

On 1 September 1939, Hitler gave the order that set 'Operation White' in motion: without a prior declaration of war, forty-eight army divisions stormed across the Polish border, while German warships blockaded the Baltic ports and 1,600 aircraft scythed down the Polish air force and dropped their bombs on Warsaw.

Hitler knew he was taking a risk. The British and French had pledged to support the Poles, and he would now face an enemy to the west while his armies were moving east. But he was confident that Poland would soon surrender — her navy was trapped in port, her air force was inadequate, her army grossly out of date with cavalry facing tanks, sabres against machine guns. With his eastern front secure, then he would deal with those tiresome Western Powers.

The Phoney War

'... I have to tell you now that no such undertaking has been received, and that consequently this country is at war with Germany.' Chamberlain's sombre pronouncement that Sunday morning, 3 September 1939, was heard on wireless sets all over the nation. In a way, the news was a relief. After months and years of convoluted but ultimately futile diplomatic manoeuvring, at least the waiting was over: war had begun.

For many Britons, the horrors of World War One were still clear in their minds. There was little doubt that this new war would be heralded by the appearance of enormous fleets of bomber aircraft raining death and destruction from the skies. The bombing of Britain by Zeppelin and aircraft during the Great War added weight to this. Theorists calculated that London could be destroyed within days. It was predicted that 'a continuous torrent of high explosives at the rate of seventy-five tons a day for an indefinite period would paralyse the War Office and the Admiralty and render London uninhabitable'. Fortunately these calculations proved totally inaccurate for they assumed, amongst other things, that all the bombs dropped would strike important targets. If this was not enough cause for concern amongst the inhabitants of the city, there was also the threat of massive poisonous gas attacks. Over thirty-five million gas masks had been distributed in September 1938, sufficient to equip every man, woman and child in the country. Air Raid Wardens made house-to-house inspections of the gas masks. This did nothing to allay the fears of the population: rather it added substance to them.

The truth was considerably more prosaic. The war began less with a bang than a whimper of apprehension. Millions of Britons fled to the air-raid shelters when sirens sounded only minutes after the Prime Minister's broadcast. It was a false alarm, however, the first of many. The country entered a strange and fearful limbo in which nothing happened. And nothing went on happening. It was the start of the so-called 'phoney war'.

While Hitler's storm troopers rampaged over eastern Europe, in Britain there reigned a nervous calm. Children were evacuated from large cities, labelled like parcels and despatched to live with strangers in the country. Shelters were dug in back gardens, offices and shops were sandbagged, the black-out was rigorously enforced by air-raid wardens with peremptory whistles. London's skies filled with barrage balloons, glinting like fat silver sausages as they tugged and swayed at their cables, while anti-aircraft guns sprouted by dockside or railway junction.

This time of limbo, tense though it was, provided the country with a chance to make good its lack of preparedness. During the summer, a chain of RDF (radio direction finding) stations had come into operation, an invaluable early-warning system that would soon be tested to the full. But the Anti-Aircraft Command and the RAF's Fighter Command were still sadly under strength when war broke out; and the latter was further weakened when four of the notional fifty-seven fighter squadrons were sent to France, followed by another two at the end of 1939. Dowding, as head of both commands, fought long and hard — as we shall see — for these shortfalls to be remedied; and slowly, belatedly, the air defences of the United Kingdom were stiffened for the fight to come.

On 14 October, a U-boat penetrated the Royal Navy's anchorage at Scapa Flow and sank HMS *Royal Oak* with the loss of 833 lives. Occasional German raiders probed the east coast of Britain, making reconnaissance flights or attacking shipping, but were detected by RDF and rapidly chased away. Otherwise there was very little enemy action. Even the RAF squadrons in France seemed becalmed in this curious hiatus in the war; the first real encounter they had with the Luftwaffe was not until 22 December, when a roving patrol of Bf.109s shot down two Hurricanes.

The war continued but at a distance. Such was the tedium that the far-off naval victory of the Battle of the River Plate, in mid-December, was celebrated in Britain with near-hysterical jubilation.

The calm before the storm would last seven months. By April 1940 Hitler's war machine was rumbling into action in the west.

A Time of Limbo

1 September 1939. German troops invade Poland. Britain announces general mobilization of armed forces; evacuation begins of three million women and children from major cities.

3 September 1939. Britain and France declare war on Germany. A French aircraft which is not immediately identifiable, not having filed a flight plan, causes the first scare: an air-raid alarm sounds within minutes of Chamberlain's broadcast.

4 September 1939. The first British troops land in France, part of the British Expeditionary Force. The BEF includes an Air Component (comprising reconnaissance aircraft and bombers, with four Hurricane squadrons), which will be supported by the Advanced Air Striking Force (AASF: initially ten squadrons of bombers, two of Hurricanes). Meanwhile, Hitler's invasion of Poland continues unchecked; despite their pledge to the Poles, the British and French are in no state to confront the well-armed Germans.

6 September 1939. The Battle of Barking Creek: identified as hostile, two Hurricanes are attacked by Spitfires from a neighbouring squadron; one is shot down and Pilot Officer Hulton-Harrop is killed.

26 September 1939. Skuas from *Ark Royal* make the first British hit on the Luftwaffe, when a Dornier flying boat is shot down in the North Sea.

28 September 1939. Poland surrenders to Germany after a gallant — and lonely — fight. But Hitler is not yet entirely committed to war in the west; clinging to the hope that Britain still wants to avoid bloodshed, he holds back from all-out war and thus gives the country a chance to repair its lack of preparedness.

14 October 1939. A U-boat torpedoes *Royal Oak* in Scapa Flow. Mines and submarines have already accounted for thousands of tons of shipping during these opening months of the war — many of the mines dropped by the Luftwaffe.

16 October 1939. The Luftwaffe's first major bombing raid on mainland Britain is carried out by nine Ju.88s over the Firth of Forth, damaging two cruisers (*Edinburgh* and *Southampton*). Spitfires shoot down two of the raiders.

17 December 1939. The Royal Navy wins the Battle of the River Plate, when the German pocket battleship *Graf Spee*, threatening Allied shipping in the South Atlantic, is forced to scuttle off Montevideo in Uruguay.

January–February 1940. A bitterly cold winter, with heavy snowfalls followed by a sudden thaw and flooding, adds to the misery of rationing and anxious anticipation.

16 March 1940. The first civilian casualty in Britain dies as a result of German action: James Isbister is killed by a bomb in the Orkneys (a prime target area for the Luftwaffe, on account of the naval anchorage at Scapa Flow). Meanwhile, in Berlin, Hitler is putting the finishing touches to his plans for the invasion of Norway, aided by the Norwegian traitor Quisling, and starting to plan the invasion of France.

The Balloon Goes Up

The stalemate came to an abrupt end on 9 April 1940 when German forces invaded Denmark and Norway. Advised by Grand Admiral Raeder (head of the Kriegsmarine, the German navy) to secure the Baltic, Hitler had unleashed his seasoned troops to the north. Denmark was soon overrun and Norway's southern ports and airfields seized. Norwegian resistance fighters and the Allies, aided by a squadron of ageing Gloster Gladiator biplanes and a clutch of Hurricanes, still held the north of Norway; but the Luftwaffe had the overwhelming advantage of numbers as well as bases. The outcome was inevitable.

Germany had invaded Norway in Operation 'Weserübung Nord' (Weser Crossing North) with six army regiments, one parachute battalion, one thousand aircraft, two battle cruisers, one pocket battleship, seven cruisers, fourteen destroyers and thirty U-boats. Against this the Norwegians fielded six army divisions, four coastal batteries, eighty aircraft, eleven small ships and nine submarines. King Maakon escaped a German trap and Vidkun Quisling proclaimed himself head of the Norwegian government, working in collaboration with Germans.

Meanwhile Hitler's attention had turned west. Just as the French had feared all along, he wanted mastery of all Europe. But the massive fortifications of the Maginot line would prove no barrier to the invaders; they merely sidestepped it. Indeed, nothing would stop these invaders. The British Expeditionary Force in northern France by this time numbered roughly a quarter of a million troops, supported by the 'Air Component' (including four Hurricane squadrons) and the AASF (Advanced Air Striking Force, comprising mainly bomber squadrons but also two of fighters). More fighter squadrons would arrive very shortly — but in vain.

On 10 May 1940 the German assault began. Again the Blitzkrieg tactics struck the defenders a mortal blow. The Stukas led the attack, dive-bombing the horrified populations of Luxembourg, Belgium and the Netherlands, while paratroops linked up with infantry to spearhead the advance. The BEF and the French First Army moved north into Belgium to meet the threat. Three panzer divisions, in a clear demonstration of the Germans' superior mobility, made an unexpected thrust through the forested hill country of the Ardennes, hitherto thought impenetrable. Then, sweeping westwards, they isolated the Allied armies on the Franco-Belgian border and started to tighten the trap.

Overhead, like the outdated French aircraft, the obsolescent Fairey Battles and even the Bristol Blenheims were easy prey for the Bf.109s, although the Messerschmitts

still faced many a furious dogfight with the battling Hurricanes. By 12 May, the number of AASF bombers had been halved. By the 14th, the Dutch air force was virtually nonexistent; on the 15th the Netherlands surrendered.

At home, Dowding was in despair. His fighter squadrons were now reduced to thirty-seven, and it was clear that they would very soon face the Luftwaffe in British skies. On 19 May, the same day that London faced the likelihood of the BEF having to be evacuated, the decision was made that no more fighters should be sent to France. On the following day, the Germans reached the Channel coast, completing the encirclement.

Suddenly Hitler had turned up the heat. Half of continental Europe was under Nazi domination and the other half looked like falling very soon. British prospects looked almost as grim. A vast expeditionary force was caught in an ever-tightening net, and, though efforts would be made to rescue them, up to four-fifths were officially expected to be lost. The German armies and above all the Luftwaffe had displayed seamless confidence and mastery of modern warfare.

Just as Britain's future looked bleakest, however, the country had acquired a new Prime Minister: Churchill.

Russia's Winter War attack
German attack
Allied reactions

Blitzkrieg in the West

28 November 1939. Russia annexes Baltic States and invades Finland in the 'Winter War'.
9 April 1940. German troops invade Denmark and southern Norway.
14 April 1940. Allied troops land in northern Norway to assist resistance fighters.
24 April 1940. A squadron of Gloster Gladiators arrives but is wiped out in days. Two further squadrons, including Hurricanes, also lost.
10 May 1940. Hitler invades the Netherlands, Belgium and Luxembourg. BEF Air Component and AASF fighters and bombers are steadily destroyed. In London, Churchill replaces Chamberlain as PM.
15 May 1940. A surprise Panzer attack bursts through Luxembourg and the Ardennes, outflanking the Maginot Line to take the Allies in the rear. The Dutch Army surrenders.
19 May 1940. Wehrmacht reaches the Channel, trapping French, Belgian and British troops along the Belgian border. Belgium surrenders. Lord Gort, commanding the BEF, requests planning for an evacuation of all Allied forces by sea.
21 May 1940. Surviving Hurricanes withdrawn from France as their bases are overrun by German advances.
26 May 1940. Operation Dynamo, the evacuation of Dunkirk, begins.

Allied lines
German advances

The Lion's Roar

On 10 May 1940, the same day that Germany launched a Blitzkrieg on the west, Prime Minister Neville Chamberlain resigned. He had been criticized for his handling of the war in Norway, and eighty Conservative MPs had rebelled against his leadership. His government was replaced by the National Coalition, including Labour and Liberal MPs, led by Winston Churchill.

Criticism of Chamberlain had reached a peak on 7 and 8 May when he was told, 'In the name of God, go!' and Lloyd George stated: 'The Prime Minister has appealed for sacrifice — he should sacrifice the Seals of Office!'. His resignation had pitched Churchill, who had served under Chamberlain as First Lord of the Admiralty, into office at a time of crisis, yet he accepted this new challenge calmly. He later wrote, 'As I went to bed at about 3.00 a.m. I was conscious of a profound sense of relief ... I felt as if I were walking with destiny and that all my past life had been in preparation for this hour and this trial ... I was sure I would not fail. Therefore, though impatient for the morning, I slept soundly.'

The new Prime Minister was uniquely qualified both by personality and by experience to unite the country in wartime. On 13 May, in a speech presenting his all-party War Cabinet to the Commons, he memorably proclaimed that he had 'nothing to offer but blood, toil, tears and sweat', then went on to stir the nation with his call for 'Victory at all costs, victory in spite of all terror, victory however long and hard the road may be; for without victory there is no survival.' Britain's ultimate survival and victory would, in fact, depend to a very large extent on this one man, whose fighting talk made such a refreshing change from the platitudes of his predecessors.

Grandson of the seventh Duke of Marlborough and son of Lord Randolph Churchill, Winston was born to a life of privilege and military prowess — though he nearly failed to gain entry to Sandhurst. His early career included action against belligerent tribesmen on India's Northwest Frontier and imprisonment as a journalist during the Boer War. Always a political maverick, he entered Parliament as a Conservative MP in 1900, then joined the Liberals in 1904, became a 'constitutional anti-socialist' in 1924 and finally rejoined the Tories in 1925.

Despite his swivelling loyalties, Churchill soon made his mark as a politician. Appointed First Lord of the Admiralty in 1911, he was instrumental in modernizing the navy and introducing an air wing in time for the First World War. After the Dardanelles débâcle in 1915, with huge loss of life, he was — unfairly — held responsible, and suffered a period of disfavour. His towering ability soon won him a reprieve, but, partly because he insistently warned of the dangers of German rearmament, he again found himself at odds with prevailing thought; as a result, he endured a lonely and frustrating ten years in the political wilderness. It was not until the late 1930s, when his opposition to appeasement found echoes both in Parliament and in the country, that he began to look like a leader. On the outbreak of war, Chamberlain returned him to the Admiralty — the news being greeted with jubilation by the navy, which flashed

Winston Leonard Spencer Churchill (1874–1965)

Born in Blenheim Palace, Woodstock, the son of Lord Randolph Churchill and American-born Jennie Jerome. Educated at Harrow and Sandhurst. Commissioned into the 4th Hussars.

Sees action on the Northwest Frontier (1896–97) and at the Battle of Omdurman (1898). As correspondent for the *Morning Post* in the Boer War (1899–1900) he is captured, escapes, and takes part in the relief of Ladysmith.

Enters Parliament as a Conservative MP (1900), but resigns over the Free Trade issue; becomes a Liberal MP (1906–22). Appointed Under-Secretary for the Colonies (1905–8) and President of the Board of Trade (1908–10). A controversial Home Secretary (1910–11), he attends the Siege of Sidney Street in person. ('It was such good fun,' he comments later.)

First Lord of the Admiralty (1911–15). After the Dardanelles fiasco he joins the Royal Scots Fusiliers and fights on the Western Front (1915–16). Recalled to power he serves in several ministerial positions until losing his seat in 1922. These include Minister of Munitions (1917), Minister of War (1918–21), Minister of Air (1919–21) and Secretary of State for the Colonies (1921–22). Re-enters Parliament in 1924 and is made Chancellor of the Exchequer (1924–29).

Out of office (1929–39) after disagreements over India, rearmament and Appeasement. Openly critical of the Government's position and attitude towards what he saw as the ever-growing menace of Nazism, he voices his opinions in Parliament and in the press. It was said that he might be the right man in war, but not in peace.

After the 'wilderness years' of 1929–39 he returns to the Admiralty until 10 May 1940, when he becomes Prime Minister. He leads the country to victory but is defeated in the 1945 election. Regains the premiership in 1951–55. Created a Knight of the Garter (1953); gains honorary US citizenship (1963). Dies 1965: after state funeral, is buried at Bladon, near Woodstock.

an immediate signal to all ships: 'Winston's back!'.

And now, just as his worst predictions were being confirmed, Churchill had become Prime Minister. He was receiving cries for aid from the Belgians, the Dutch and the French, while at the same time grappling with the increasing likelihood of an invasion of mainland Britain. Lord Gort, head of the BEF, was pleading for more Hurricanes; Dowding, head of Fighter Command, was begging to keep them in reserve. Such dilemmas were the daily lot of a wartime prime minister, however, and Churchill embraced them as his destiny. Steady of nerve and clear of mind, with a quick and penetrating grasp of matters both general and specific, he rattled out decisions in terms as lucid as succinct. And yet, although sometimes irascible and daunting to his colleagues, he never lost the common touch, the ability to share the pain and pride of ordinary people. Over the air waves or in the House, he steadied the country for the emergency ahead.

Very soon Churchill would have stamped his authority on the war. With that V-for-victory sign, that fat cigar and bulldog growl, he embodied defiance towards the Nazis. 'I may not be the British Lion,' he once said, 'but I am privileged to be its roar!'

AOC-in-C

If Churchill's leadership was a major asset to Britain, an equal contribution was made by men like Air Chief Marshal Sir Hugh Dowding, Air Officer Commanding-in-Chief of Fighter Command.

Dowding discovered the joys of flying in 1912, after twelve years' service with the Royal Artillery. He was attending a Staff College course at Camberley when he realized that few senior officers had grasped the potential of aviation, and decided to take flying lessons himself. He won his 'ticket' after less than two hours in the air, then had his expenses reimbursed by the War Office who now sent him to the Central Flying School. Thus qualified, he was propelled into the Royal Flying Corps at the outbreak of war in 1914, and sent to command a squadron in France.

Dowding ended the war a brigadier general, then joined the new RAF in 1918 as an air commodore responsible for training and reserves. Throughout the 1920s he maintained a close interest in technical development, which earned him a place on the Air Council in 1930. But now Dowding ran into blinkered prejudice. The two most vital innovations at this time were monoplanes and metal construction; in both instances, Dowding had to overcome extreme official scepticism. It was he who fostered the advance of the Hurricane and Spitfire; and, just as important, it was he, as the RAF's head of research and development, who gave official momentum to the 1935 experiments that would result in radar.

A tall, rather austere man, noted for integrity rather than bonhomie, Dowding's brushes with politicians and civil servants did not earn him friends in high places; indeed, he angered many with his acid tongue. As a result, when the RAF was reorganized in 1936, he was given Fighter Command: a subtle depreciation by officialdom which then regarded bombers as supreme.

From the first, however, Dowding worked to prove officialdom wrong. He arrived at Bentley Priory, his new headquarters near Stanmore in Middlesex, on 14 July 1936. By this time Hitler had sent troops into the Rhineland, and Spain was on the verge of convulsion; to a realist such as Dowding there was no escaping a world war now. Building on the foundations laid by Trenchard — a man whose views he had not always shared — he created a strong and reliable fighter defence force. He supervised the development not only of modern aircraft, but of the early-warning system and communications network combining both radar and the Observer Corps. Struggling against economies and political restraints, he won armour-plating and bullet-proof windscreens for his fighters; more airfields, some with hard runways; and always more aircraft, more squadrons, more pilots.

In September 1939, excluding the four squadrons sent to France, Dowding had thirty-five fighter squadrons: seventeen of Hurricanes, twelve of Spitfires, the rest a motley collection of biplanes. But by now Fighter Command's duties included protection for east coast convoys, and Dowding grew ever more anxious about the dwindling numbers of aircraft available for front-line defence; as more and more Hurricanes disappeared abroad, he feared for the nation's chances in the event of an invasion. His persistent arguing finally won him the support of Air Chief Marshal Sir Cyril Newall, the

The outcome of the Battle of Britain was determined at a meeting in the Cabinet Room of No. 10 Downing Street on the evening of 15th May, when Dowding persuaded Churchill that Britain could not afford to lose more fighter aircraft in France.

Chief of Air Staff, who ordered production of Hurricanes and Spitfires to be stepped up. By March 1940 Dowding had another twelve squadrons — a total of forty-seven. But not for long.

First in Norway, then in northern France, Dowding's squadrons fought gallantly but against colossal odds. Desperate to halt what he saw as a squandering of resources, on 15 May he addressed the War Cabinet in person, and, speaking with all the reasoned eloquence at his command, expressed his absolute reluctance to part with even one more Hurricane. In case this did not persuade them, he then recorded his view that 'If the Home Defence force is drained away ... defeat in France will involve the final, complete and irremediable defeat of this country.' His point was taken. On 19 May, Churchill ordered that no more fighters should go to France.

During this time he was, however, fighting a more personal battle, the enemy on this occasion being the Air Ministry itself. In April 1940 Hugh Dowding was fifty-eight years of age and would normally have been retired before that age. The authorities had repeatedly extended his tenure of office by a few weeks here and a month there. This was obviously far from satisfactory. On 6 July he was exasperated to receive yet another letter deferring his retirement, but only until the end of October. In his letter of reply he pointed out that this was the fifth change of retirement date so far and asked if it would not be possible for him to remain Air Officer Commander-in-Chief, Fighter Command until the end of the war. Nothing was formally agreed but he did win sufficient time to concentrate on the affairs in hand.

Father of the Few

Air Chief Marshal Sir Hugh Caswell Tremenheere Dowding, GCB, GCVO, CMG (later first Baron Dowding of Bentley Priory).

Born in Moffat, Scotland, on 24 April 1882, the son of a preparatory school headmaster. Educated at Winchester and the Royal Military Academy, Woolwich. Commissioned (1900) into the Royal Garrison Artillery. While on a Staff College course at Camberley, Surrey, he develops an interest in aviation and learns to fly (1912). Having honed his skills with the RFC at Upavon, in 1914 he takes No. 16 Squadron to France.

Promoted to brigadier general, he marries (1918) and fathers a son (born 1919) but is widowed in 1920. By now an air commodore with the new RAF, his duties include organizing the Hendon air displays. After two years as Chief of Staff in Iraq he is appointed to the Air Ministry, joining the Air Council (1930) where his open-minded support for modern technology outweighs official prejudice.

In 1936 he is created Air Chief Marshal, AOC-in-C of Fighter Command, and urgently promotes the fighter control and interception systems that will prove crucial during the Battle of Britain.

Retires November 1940, is recalled 1941, retires again 1942. Ennobled 1943. Remarries 1951. Dies 1970.

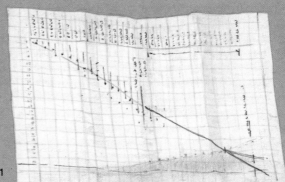

Dunkirk

The French First Army and BEF were caught in the panzers' pincer-grip. On 19 May Lord Gort warned London that the only way out of this trap was by sea. On the 20th the War Cabinet asked Vice-Admiral Sir Bertram Ramsay, C-in-C Dover, to prepare an evacuation plan under the codename of Operation Dynamo.

Ramsay's task was gigantic, yet very simple. Hundreds of thousands of troops were to be collected from a foreign shore where enemy activity could be expected. The Royal Navy, the Merchant Navy, auxiliary and reserve fleets, cross-Channel ferries and fishing boats would all help; but still Ramsay wasn't satisfied. He summoned reinforcements in the form of tugs, barges, private motor launches and yachts — anything seaworthy, no matter how small. On the night of the 26th, Operation Dynamo began. The raggle-taggle armada set off across the Channel to Dunkirk.

Meanwhile, in northern France, while the ground forces retreated towards the coast in considerable disorder (although there were brave last ditch stands by some rearguards), the Hurricanes kept up their unequal battle against the Luftwaffe. Vastly outnumbered, they flew a constant round of sorties to intercept the German bombers and fighters. And their efforts were by no means unrewarded; in the ten days to 20 May they had shot down an estimated 350 enemy aircraft. In the same period, seventy-five Hurricanes had been lost in action — but another 120 had been lost on the ground, as Allied airbases were either overrun or destroyed by bombs. On the 21st, the decision was made to withdraw most

squadrons to English bases. Henceforth they would operate from across the Channel.

Mysteriously, the German tanks drew to a halt on 23 May. While the noose tightened on the retreating armies, it had seemed that they would be annihilated before they could escape. But the order to halt came from Hitler himself, possibly because he wanted to preserve his panzers for an all-out assault later and Göring boasted that the Luftwaffe could complete the job. Hitler's reasons are unclear, but the upshot was a two-day easing of pressure on the Allied force.

In the early hours of 27 May the evacuation began. Streams of khaki-clad soldiers boarded the haphazard collection of ships and boats at Dunkirk port itself and along nearby beaches. And among the khaki was a growing band of blue: fighter pilots shot down inside the beachhead. Contrary to the soldiers' muttered complaints that the RAF had abandoned them, Fighter Command was now meeting the Luftwaffe face to face. Dowding had authorized his senior commander, Air Vice-Marshal Keith Park, not merely to fly covering patrols for the troops but to escort bombing raids against the enemy. On the 27th alone, No. 11 Group made over 250 sorties from southeast England, and among the battle-weary Hurricanes for the first time there were Spitfires. On the following days, the sorties increased in both number and strength.

But the aerial combatants were hidden by low cloud cover. The troops knew only that those clouds would suddenly part to reveal a Junkers Ju.87 with siren screaming, dive-bombing the ships in the

Above: The classical elements combine against troops waiting for rescue at Dunkirk. Water, as they wade into the sea. Fire, as bombs explode around them. Air, compressed by bomb-blast, which hurls them to the ground and deafens them. Earth, or sand, filling the mouths of the dead.

port, or a Messerschmitt Bf.109 streaking over the beach with machine guns chattering, leaving death in its wake. Afterwards the throng of waiting men would pick themselves off the ground and patiently reform their disciplined lines, endlessly shuffling towards the harbour mole where a Thames lighter, perhaps, was arriving to collect them; or wading shoulder-deep into the sea and heaving themselves wearily into a bobbing dinghy that would transfer them to a paddle-steamer from Southend.

Day after day the evacuation continued; but all the time the pressure was increasing. On the 28th, Belgium surrendered and the enemy was able to concentrate attention on the south. The heroic rearguard units, mainly French, managed to hold the shrinking perimeter until 1 June. By this time, most of the BEF troops had been evacuated, but there still remained thousands of French, Belgian, Dutch and other Allied soldiers. On the morning of 2 June, Park's squadrons engaged the enemy in a last furious battle, successfully warding off German attacks on the retreating ships. The following two days were swathed in mist: neither air force was able to fly. On the afternoon of 4 June, Operation Dynamo was concluded: the Dunkirk perimeter had collapsed and the remaining troops surrendered.

A third of a million men had been snatched from the jaws of Nazi captivity: men who would fight again. It was undoubtedly a cause for rejoicing, despite the countervailing losses and the abandonment of much heavy equipment. But the cost to Fighter Command had been immense. Air Chief Marshal Dowding's carefully husbanded resources had been virtually halved, just when a German invasion of Britain looked imminent.

Counting the Cost

In the nine days to 4 June 1940, a total of 338,226 troops were evacuated from Dunkirk. A remarkable feat — but the cost was high. Untold thousands of Allied soldiers had lost their lives or their liberty. Tanks, guns, ammunition had to be abandoned. And, since 10 May, the RAF had lost 944 aircraft, including 386 Hurricanes and 67 Spitfires, and 915 aircrew of whom 435 were experienced pilots. The evacuation itself had cost 243 vessels sunk out of the 860 used, including one AA cruiser and six destroyers, with another nineteen destroyers being damaged.

Below: The Allied lines (green) on **(1)** 22 May and **(2)** 25 May. The Dunkirk perimeter on **(3)** 29 May and **(4)** 1 June. Red: Wehrmacht advances. Blue: Allied escape routes.

43

Respite

As the last boat left Dunkirk on 4 June, Britain braced herself for invasion. If it had seemed inevitable before, now it was surely imminent. The Nazi forces were massed just across the Channel, less than twenty-five miles away. The Luftwaffe was installed in air bases within easy striking distance of southern Britain. No doubt the Wehrmacht officers were focusing their field glasses on the white cliffs and joking among themselves: We'll be in Soho by the weekend... Let's have tea at the Ritz...

Churchill's grim speech to the House of Commons that same day, 4 June, merely confirmed what the country was expecting. 'We shall defend our island, whatever the cost may be,' he thundered. 'We shall fight on the beaches ... on the landing grounds ... in the fields and in the streets ... we shall never surrender.' Bold and stirring words; but the Germans would not be coming just yet.

The day after they captured Dunkirk (along with 40,000 French troops and all the abandoned BEF equipment) the Wehrmacht launched 'Operation Red'. Storming south across the river Somme, Hitler's troops overwhelmed the French defence. The Luftwaffe met continued resistance from Dowding's fighters, which now became increasingly busy at home, too, as British air space was daily invaded by enemy reconnaissance aircraft; but on the ground the German advance was relentless. The French had fortified villages and erected road blocks but, by 6 June, Rommel had broken through at Amiens and advanced 20 miles (32km). The next day Panzers pushed on another 30 miles (48km) and by 13 June were on the outskirts of Paris. British forces from

further south in France made an orderly evacuation through northern ports, covered by Hurricane squadrons now based in the Channel Islands. All too soon it was over.

On 14 June the Germans took Paris. On the 17th Marshal Pétain, a hero in the First World War, led the call for an armistice. Hitler reportedly did a jig of triumph. Still nursing resentment at the shame heaped on Germany twenty-two years before, he sent for the very railway carriage in which the November 1918 armistice had been signed, and had it brought to the same spot at Compiègne. Now it was his turn to inflict humiliation. The French nation surrendered on 22 June. Since Norway had finally surrendered on the 10th, Britain and the Commonwealth now stood alone in the fight against Nazism.

On the 18th Churchill had solemnly warned: 'The Battle for France is over. I expect that the Battle for Britain is about to begin.' That very night there was a major Luftwaffe attack on military and communications targets ranging from Hampshire to Yorkshire. Yet even now the German land forces delayed their invasion of Britain. They were breathless at the speed of their own advance; they needed to consolidate, to regroup, both literally and metaphorically. Although French air bases had been seized by the Luftwaffe's spearhead forces, now the administrators moved in to organize supply lines, communications, facilities for personnel and all the rest of the efficient infrastructure on which this military élite depended.

Across the Channel, frantic last-minute arrangements were made to repel the invaders. No one doubted now that they were coming. 'Let us therefore brace ourselves to our duty,' the Prime Minister had said on 18 June, 'and so bear ourselves that if the British Commonwealth and Empire lasts for a thousand years men will still say, "This was their finest hour".' But these weeks of hectic activity would later be looked back on as a time of grace, a 'magic month' that enabled Fighter Command to rehabilitate the squadrons so heavily depleted in France.

Indeed, it was not merely the fighter squadrons that benefited from this breathing space. Thanks to provocative daily visits by Luftwaffe teams reconnoitring and testing UK defences, the radar operators, Observer Corps and fighter controllers were acquiring valuable operational expertise, as were AA Command and Civil Defence — the latter now reorganized on a national basis.

The chief benefit, however, was undoubtedly to Dowding's fighters. During the past few weeks they had suffered terrible losses. The loss of Hurricanes and Spitfires was grievous, but aircraft are replaceable. Already, thanks to the efforts of Lord Beaverbrook, the production industry was starting to function at a more effective level, and dozens of new aircraft were joining the fighter squadrons every day. Pilots are less easy to replace. Dowding persuaded Churchill to authorize the release of pilots from other services, including the Fleet Air Arm, Bomber Command and Coastal Command, and efforts were intensified to train new men and retrain the pilots from France, Poland, Czechoslovakia and other occupied nations who had found their way to England. Manpower was still a nagging worry to Dowding, who knew the pitiable truth that no one could fully replace the experienced professionals lost in Europe, but at least the numerical shortfall was being reduced.

On the credit side, Fighter Command now knew that its Hurricanes and Spitfires were a match for the enemy's fighters. They had acquired experience of combat — and the scars to prove it — and the Luftwaffe pilots had lost much of their overweening self-assurance. Moreover, as the forthcoming battle would be fought out in British skies, Dowding's Command possessed one enormous asset: a highly advanced technological picture of, and control of, fighters in the sky.

The Fall of France

5 June 1940. German forces enter Dunkirk.

7 June 1940. French demands for RAF support, in addition to the three AASF fighter squadrons still in France, result in Dowding losing another two Hurricane squadrons; based just south of the river Seine, they are soon forced westwards by the German advance.

13 June 1940. Churchill flies to Tours in a last desperate attempt to persuade the French leaders to stand fast. In vain.

14 June 1940. Fall of Paris. The French government flees south in disarray, while a new government is formed under Marshal Pétain, the 'victor of Verdun' (where he halted a German advance in 1916), now aged eighty-four and destined for notoriety as head of the puppet régime formally instituted on 1 July at the spa town of Vichy.

17 June 1940. Pétain, the right-wing authoritarian marshal and former war hero, surrenders France to the Nazis.

18 June 1940. The last British troops leave Europe following an orderly withdrawal through Britanny and Normandy.

21 June 1940. The last surviving Hurricanes, vastly outnumbered and pushed westwards and northwards to the Channel Islands, finally return home.

22 June 1940. The French sign the armistice at Compiègne, following which Hitler returns to Germany in triumph to finalize his invasion plan for Britain.

28 June 1940. German bombs rain down on the Channel Islands, killing twenty-nine: the first enemy raid involving major loss of life on British soil.

Control

To alert the country to the intrusion of enemy aircraft, attempts had been made, ever since the First World War, to create an early-warning system in Britain. Defence of the skies could not rely wholly on RAF patrols, and the sound-location scheme considered in the early 1920s was inadequate. It was Dowding, as the RAF's head of research, who in 1934 persuaded the Air Ministry to set up a committee — headed by Henry Tizard, a former pilot and a distinguished scientist — to evaluate the latest scientific experiments using radio.

Wireless telegraphy, the transmission and reception of radio signals, had been developed by the Italian physicist Marconi in 1895. Forty years later, science was playing with the idea of 'death rays': radio waves that could somehow be used to incapacitate a pilot or aircraft. Robert Watson-Watt, of the Radio Research Laboratory at Slough, soon dismissed the death-ray idea, but indicated that radio waves did have potential as a means of detecting aircraft. Recent investigation had shown that it was possible to locate a thunderstorm by transmitting radio waves and measuring the time it took for the reflected waves to return. The same principle might prove effective with aircraft.

Dowding's committee asked Watson-Watt for a demonstration, and the results — on 26 February 1935 — were so convincing that Dowding immediately made funds available for further research. The project was called 'Radio Direction Finding' (RDF), later renamed 'radio location', and finally, in 1943, adopting the American abbreviation for RAdio Detecting And Ranging, acquired the name by which it is known today: 'radar'.

By the end of 1935 the project had become reality. A chain of RDF stations was being built around Britain's coast. Each station would comprise a powerful transmitter mast 360ft high and a 240ft receiver tower, the latter being linked to a cathode-ray screen that displayed a recording of the reflected wave, or echo, as an irregularity or 'blip'. The first station was operating by mid-March 1936, at Orfordness in Suffolk; by the outbreak of war the chain numbered twenty.

Radar worked by night as well as by day, regardless of weather conditions. It could detect an aircraft 100 miles away or more, and show its bearing and approximate altitude. Later refinements in 1939 included IFF (Identification Friend or Foe), a small transponder in the aircraft which created a distinctive shape of blip and thus enabled operators to distinguish between friendly and hostile aircraft; and Pipsqueak, a device attached to the aircraft's RT which emitted a periodic signal, allowing its course to be plotted.

'Hello Maidstone, Observer Corps K3, Beachy Head. Raid approaching Area 8723. Estimated forty-plus — hang on ... He.111s, escorted by God knows how many Messerschmitts stacked above. I reckon more than forty. Bombers at about 11,000 feet, course 290 degrees.' 'OK, it confirms plot 235.'

'Rye HC. Blip indicating forty-plus bandits. Range seventy miles, direction 110 degrees. There's a build-up over the Pas de Calais. I think they're coming this way.' 'OK, Rye, plot 235.'

By early 1940 the radar stations were staffed mainly by specially trained WAAFS. Hunched over the screen, the operator was usually accompanied by one or more 'tellers' who relayed the information by telephone to Group Headquarters or indeed to Stanmore. Here it would pass through a 'filter room' where the information was assessed, collated with other reports arriving from Observer Corps, and passed on to the 'ops room' for 'plotters' to display using markers on a large map table. Continually updated, this graphic display enabled the senior controller at Group or Sector HQ to decide where and when to send his fighters, and how many; he would relay his instructions to the squadron or directly to the pilots in the air by means of a simple code: 'Scramble' meaning take off; 'Bandits' meaning enemy raiders; 'Angels 20' meaning at a height of 20,000ft, etc.

Although Germany had her own equivalent of radar, it was used only for shipping; the Luftwaffe remained ignorant, until after the Battle of Britain, of the real purpose for that network of tall masts sprouting around England's shore. And Hermann Göring's pilots would grow daily more baffled at the RAF's consistent ability to intercept the raiders.

'Tally-ho!'

'Gimlet Squadron, scramble. Buster on Vector 95 to patrol, angels twenty over Maidstone. Escorts stacked up above you, but go for the bombers. Kiwi Squadron will deal with the escort.'

Plots are now passed on to sector stations and duplicated on sector Ops Room table *(above)*. Sector controllers talk directly to air leaders over RT.

11 Group HQ, Hillingdon, Middlesex

10 Group HQ, Box Hill, Somerset

12 Group HQ, Watnall

13 Group HQ, Newcastle

Reports pass on to Fighter Command HQ where Filter Room removes friendly aircraft or mistaken reports. Raid 235 is plotted on the table. Positions are passed on to Group HQ and responses added as reported.

Range limit of Chain Home

HQ 13 Group

HQ 12 Group

HQ 10 Group

HQ 11 Group

HQ Fighter Command Stanmore

Range limit of Chain Home Low

Reichsmarschall

In the early summer of 1940 Hermann Göring was at the peak of his career. Apart from being deputy chancellor of the Reich and a close confidant of the Führer, he was head of the Air Ministry and commander-in-chief of the Luftwaffe. In July he was created *Reichsmarschall* ('Empire Marshal'), a unique rank signalling Hitler's approbation of his achievements. But success had gone to Göring's head. Indeed, it can be argued that his overweening belief in himself and his Luftwaffe contributed directly to the postponement of the assault on Britain.

Göring was twenty-four years of age when the First World War began and by this time he had already been a commissioned officer in the infantry for two years. In 1915 he left the trenches to join the rapidly expanding air force. He reached the rank of Hauptmann in 1918 and commanded the fighter unit *Jagdgeschwader 1*, which had been led by the legendary Baron Manfred von Richthofen.

Göring's glittering prowess as a fighter pilot during the First World War left him ill-prepared for the debased military status of post-war Germany. Forbidden even to set foot on a German airfield, he went to Sweden, where he worked as a commercial pilot and aircraft salesman and met his first wife. Meanwhile, an Austrian-born former corporal was sowing the seeds of the future Reich, and on returning to his homeland Göring became attracted to the cause. Like Hitler he had taken Germany's defeat as a personal insult; like Hitler he dreamed of a disciplined nation rising out of the ashes of humiliation; like Hitler he loathed Jews.

Following the failure of the Munich putsch, Göring fled abroad; but his destiny was fused with Hitler's. He was elected to the Reichstag in 1928; five years later he was not only President but also Reich Air Minister, with overall control of the secretly burgeoning Luftwaffe. By the outbreak of the Second World War, he commanded the most powerful and best equipped air force in the world. The Luftwaffe's undoubted success in Spain, Poland and now France gave the former fighter pilot — still aged just forty-six — due cause for pride; nothing, however, could have justified the soaring conceit that he now displayed. His swaggering provoked both ridicule and resentment, but criticism was muted, for this man had Hitler's ear.

Along with power and influence Göring had acquired a taste for the soft life: fine art, jewels, rich food — and drugs, for he was addicted to cocaine. He designed his own flamboyant uniforms, evidently unashamed of his barrel-like shape which had earned him the nickname of *der Dicke* ('Fatty'). He was wont to overrule his subordinates' decisions at a moment's notice, interfering with their careful plans, demanding changes in strategy and then growing impatient at their protestations. He began to feel himself invincible. But in his arrogance Göring failed to believe his own pilots when they reported the RAF's impressive performance, not only in European air space but in British skies too. It was easier for him to think they were lying than that his Luftwaffe could be matched, even outdone, by the RAF.

He scoffed at those like his own second-in-

command, Erhard Milch, and Albert Kesselring, one of his senior commanders, who argued that now was the time to strike, while Britain was still reeling from the humiliation of Dunkirk. Recklessly he continued to brag: that the RAF would be destroyed in three weeks; that Britain could be made to surrender merely by bombing London; that air supremacy belonged to the Luftwaffe. And his boasts helped to convince Hitler that the invasion of Britain could safely be deferred.

The plans for the invasion, codenamed Operation Sealion (*Seelöwe*), were well in hand by now. It is not inconceivable that if the assault had begun immediately after Dunkirk, when the RAF was reeling from its losses, the Luftwaffe would indeed have won air supremacy. However, in June 1940 Göring believed there was no urgency. While Dowding goaded Fighter Command into ever greater efforts, his German counterpart lingered comfortably over preparations for the battle ahead. Late that month, arriving in northern France in his luxurious private train — specially ballasted to give a smooth ride — Göring issued leisurely orders for the *Kanalkampf* ('Channel War'). This series of skirmishes over the Channel was intended to be a preliminary stage in the air assault, to weaken the RAF both numerically and psychologically while the Luftwaffe built up its new bases opposite the south coast of England. And, basking in his new rank of Reichsmarschall, Göring would continue to ignore reality for weeks to come. The British, on the other hand, were grimly exploiting this unexpected hiatus in the Nazi advance.

Hermann Wilhelm Göring

Born on 12 January 1893 in Rosenheim, Bavaria, Göring grew up in Veldenstein, near Nuremberg, where his mother (with his father's acquiescence) slept with their wealthy Jewish landlord. Commissioned in 1912, Göring was an infantry officer at the start of the Great War, but left the army for the flying service in 1915. By the end of the war he had claimed twenty-two victories as a fighter pilot, commanded von Richthofen's 'Flying Circus', and won the highest award for bravery. After the war he made a fitful living in Sweden, but in 1920 returned to Germany to study at Munich University. At this time he met Hitler and his fate was sealed.

1922 — joins the Nazi party; is given command of the Storm Troopers (*Sturm-Abteilung*) or 'Brownshirts'. Marries Karin von Rosen, a Swedish countess.

1923 — wounded during the Munich putsch, he flees abroad to seek treatment in exile; becomes addicted to drugs.

1927 — returns to Germany where Nazis are gaining popular support. His war reputation and contacts in aviation are invaluable to Hitler, who persuades him to stand for election.

1928 — enters Reichstag. Over the next five years he works tirelessly for Hitler, establishing the Gestapo and concentration camps in order to suppress opposition.

1933 — is appointed Air Minister, with overall command of the Luftwaffe.

1935 — marries actress Emmy Sonnemann (Karin having died in 1931), who bears him a daughter. Pleading ill health, he retreats whenever possible to his luxurious estate, Karinhall, named after his first wife.

1940 — following the success of the May Blitzkrieg, he is created Reichsmarschall.

Rebuilding

Air Chief Marshal Sir Hugh Dowding, as we have seen, had fought long and hard to get an adequate number of fighter aircraft. It was galling to see his Hurricanes and Spitfires sent across the Channel to confront the more numerous Luftwaffe, weakening the home defence that he had so carefully built up. In May 1940, however, he had suddenly acquired an unlikely ally: Lord Beaverbrook, the Press baron.

One of Churchill's earliest moves, on becoming premier, had been to create a new Ministry for Air Production, and on 14 May Beaverbrook had been appointed the Minister. A short, ebullient man, Beaverbrook was Dowding's opposite in temperament as well as physique, but the two worked well together and became close friends. Dowding respected 'the Beaver's' energy and results; Beaverbrook trusted Dowding's dedication and experience. Dowding wrote later: 'The country owes as much to Beaverbrook for winning the Battle of Britain as to me.' For it was the Canadian-born newspaper magnate who so boosted aircraft production, aided by a grimly industrious workforce, that Dowding's Fighter Command eventually made up the numerical losses suffered in France.

Beaverbrook's talents had already earned him a fortune when he arrived in Britain at the age of thirty-one. Possessed of a lucid mind and the ruthlessness to apply logical decisions, he now swept through the Air Ministry's red tape as once he had swept through Canadian cement mills. Setting up office at home, he co-opted aircraft engineers and administrators, typists and telephonists, and set about his task of increasing aircraft production. A notice over his desk read: 'Organization is the enemy of improvization.'

First he assessed priorities. Production, he declared, must concentrate all available resources on five types of aircraft, two of which would be the Hurricane and the Spitfire. Next he pinpointed obstructions. One was at Castle Bromwich, Birmingham, where a new factory had been set up to make Spitfires: as yet, not a single aircraft had been made. Beaverbrook telephoned Castle Bromwich and told the factory managers bluntly: 'Build aircraft.' They did. By mid-June, their first Spitfire was rolling off the line. Now he cast an imperious eye over the Central Repair Organization (CRO), a collection of workshops and factories run by Lord Nuffield's car engineers, whose job was to patch up all but the most severely damaged aircraft. The CRO was atrophied, Beaverbrook decided, and in need or reorganization. He personally supervised the creation of a newly effective network of repair units, which could collect damaged aircraft, mend them with parts salvaged from those beyond repair and fly them back to their bases for another encounter with the enemy.

Thanks to Beaverbrook's efforts — and, it must be said, to a new sense of realism prevailing in

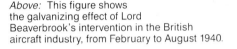

Above: This figure shows the galvanizing effect of Lord Beaverbrook's intervention in the British aircraft industry, from February to August 1940.

Britain after the Nazi conquest of Europe — the aircraft production industry was transformed. By the end of May, 325 new fighter aircraft were built, an increase of twenty-five per cent over estimates for the month. In June the output was 446, or fifty per cent higher than the estimates; in July and August it rose to 496 and 476 respectively, and as the months passed the production graph would continue to soar. Moreover, the repair units would contribute an estimated sixty per cent of the aircraft involved in the Battle of Britain. At last Dowding could field the fifty-four operational fighter squadrons that he considered an essential minimum for the nation's defence. But one problem that even Beaverbrook could not solve was how to speed up the training of new pilots.

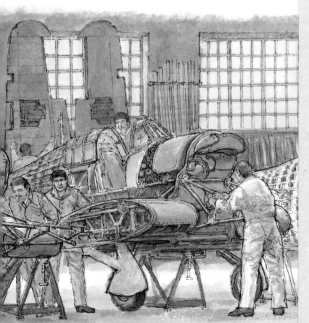

'The Beaver'

Lord Beaverbrook, born William Maxwell Aitken in Canada in 1879, had made a fortune in the cement industry before emigrating to Britain in 1910. Three months later he was a Conservative MP. Knighted in 1911 and created a baron in 1917, he built a newspaper empire around the *Daily Express* which he bought in 1917. Through his papers he campaigned vigorously for right-wing values, and led calls for appeasement. When war broke out, however, he adopted a staunchly patriotic stance. Churchill appointed him Minister of Aircraft Production in 1940. Almost overnight, his

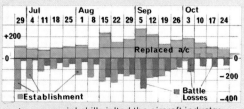

entrepreneurial skills jolted the aircraft industry into new productivity. He died in 1964, his newspaper empire inherited by his son Max, a fighter pilot in the Battle of Britain.

Dowding's Chicks

Tragically, 445 British pilots had been lost in the vain attempt to halt the Nazi whirlwind in Europe. By standing firm against French demands for yet more air support, Dowding had managed to preserve at least some of his fighter pilots, but in mid-June 1940 he estimated that he still needed a total of 360 to make up the full establishment of 1456. In effect, the shortfall amounted to sixteen squadrons of pilots.

Churchill, as we have seen *(pages 44–45)*, responded to Dowding's urgent requests by authorizing the release of pilots from the Fleet Air Arm and other commands; this produced roughly another hundred pilots, including many from the Commonwealth and Dominions and survivors from the Dutch, Belgian, French, Polish, Czech and other air forces who had managed to escape from occupied Europe. Even the best of them, however, needed to undergo cross-training before they could fly the Hurricanes and Spitfires of Fighter Command; those with combat experience would be given a hurried few hours of instruction, then posted to a new squadron. The rest would require more intensive retraining.

Dowding's problem now was that pilot training schools had not yet adapted to the realities of air combat in the 1940s. Their courses were still too leisurely, lasting as long as a year: pilots who qualified in June 1940 had been peace-time volunteers. And, although selection procedures were broadened somewhat on the outbreak of war, recruits still tended to be chosen for their social background and sporting prowess as much as their aptitude for flying a modern fighter aircraft. Like the selection boards, the training schools were too often manned by dogmatic second-raters, men who were overly impressed by class and other irrelevancies, whose instruction courses were designed to teach combat tactics that were twenty years out of date. First Trenchard, then Dowding had struggled to persuade the schools of modern requirements — but not until now were the lessons learned. Survivors from the dogfights over Europe gave weary but illuminating accounts of combat, emphasizing the enemy's expertise. Suddenly, at last, the urgency of Britain's need communicated itself to the training schools, triggering a spate of new trainees.

The recruits still faced the inevitable processes that would turn them from civilians into servicemen: parades, drill, 'bull' (for bullshit) and a seemingly pointless emphasis on spit-and-polish that in fact promoted discipline. Most of the recruits had volunteered because of a fascination with aircraft or just flying itself — usually confirmed by their first 'air familiarity' flight in a fabric-covered wire-braced biplane with an open cockpit. But their enthusiasm was soon tested to the limit by the dreary freezing hours spent practising: repeated take-offs and landings, circuits and bumps, spins, stalls and aerobatics, forced landings and 'recoveries from unusual attitude'. Back on the ground they faced even longer and drearier hours of study. Theory of flight. Navigation. Aircraft and engines. Instrument flying. Gunnery. Tactics. The desk work seemed endless.

Gradually they would gain those 'educated hands and feet', passing each hurdle in turn. The first solo flight, after eight or ten hours in a dual-control aircraft. The move to intermediate training after perhaps ten weeks of basic work. More theory. Conversion to faster single-seat or twin-engine trainers. Advance training, yet more theory, exams — and finally the passing-out parade where each survivor was awarded the coveted 'wings'. Nor was this the end. A further six weeks would be spent at an Operational Training Unit, converting to Hurricanes or Spitfires, each man slowly gaining confidence in his ability to fly these most modern of fighter aircraft, and to wield their armaments to best effect.

They were the lucky ones, the early ones. Later on, recruits were rushed through training school at a crazy rate. As the pressure of battle losses mounted, so the training courses were shortened. Some pilots would arrive at their operational squadron with scarcely a few hours' experience of monoplanes, like learner drivers forced to join the Grand Prix. Painfully aware of their novice status, despite the camaraderie that soon enveloped them, they would lap up the wisdom of the 'old stagers'. Some could profit from a quiet spell to spend a day's intensive training, with mock dogfights and interceptions, aerobatics and air-shooting, taught by those who had already 'mixed it'. Others did not even have that chance. Pilots were being pushed to their limits and as a result mistakes, sometimes fatal ones, were made. It was all too easy to forget to lower one's undercarriage, or to select the right propeller pitch, but with luck a trainee could get away with it and only wreck an aircraft. On the other hand to stall on approach and spin-in was invariably fatal.

Dowding had done his best. He had saved as many as possible of his experienced, professional fighter pilots from the early skirmishes in Europe. He had raged and pleaded and argued for more pilots, better training. He had made full use of the 'magic month', the time of respite, reorganizing Fighter Command and preparing for the real fight to come. He now assessed his surviving fighter pilots and promoted the most experienced to positions of command, where they could pass on their hard-won combat skills. They were still young men, most in their early twenties; and they had the power of life and death in their hands. Churchill called them 'Dowding's chicks'. There were not enough of them, but they would do.

The RAF

Squadrons. On 7 July 1940 Fighter Command had 54 operational squadrons, of which 26 flew Hurricanes, 19 Spitfires, and 9 twin-engined Blenheims or single-engined Defiant turret fighters. A peace-time squadron had an establishment of 18 aircraft and 22 pilots; however, due to losses sustained up to July, this was now reduced to 14 aircraft and 18 pilots.

Personnel. RAF recruits divided into officers, who were said to 'receive the King's Commission', and non-officers, usually called 'other ranks'. Every recruit, on swearing allegiance to the King, thereupon submitted to the disciplinary codes popularly known as 'KRs' and 'ACIs', the King's Regulations and the Air Council Instructions, which governed every conceivable aspect of service life (subject, of course, to civilian law).

Training. Lawyers, doctors and priests were recruited as officers on the strength of their degrees, but all officers faced specialist training in one particular branch: chiefly Pilot or General Duties; Engineering; Administration. Other ranks were recruited as 'tradesmen', likewise specializing in one particular skill: Aircraft Fitting, Engine Fitting, Electrics, Wireless, Armoury or Signals.

Commissioned officers:
RAF ranks and Army equivalents

RAF rank	Army equivalent
Pilot Officer	Second Lieutenant
Flying Officer	Lieutenant
Flight Lieutenant	Captain
Squadron Leader	Major
Wing Commander	Lieutenant-Colonel
Group Captain	Colonel
Air Commodore	Brigadier
Air Vice-Marshal	Major-General
Air Marshal	Lieutenant-General
Air Chief Marshal	General
Marshal of the RAF	Field Marshal

Gegen England

June 1940, the month of respite that proved so beneficial to Dowding, was a time of suspense for certain German officers — in the Wehrmacht and Kriegsmarine as well as the Luftwaffe. The army and navy chiefs expected almost daily to receive Hitler's orders for the invasion of Britain, and revised their plans accordingly. For his part, Göring's deputy, Erhard Milch, had personally flown over the Dunkirk evacuation scene before the last of the little boats had left, and concluded that Britain's forces were already in shambles: now was the time to strike. The mighty Germans had bundled the British out of Europe; the litter of abandoned equipment at Dunkirk told its own sorry tale. If German bombers and airborne troops could now carry the fight across the Channel, they would surely meet little opposition.

But Milch's urgings fell on deaf ears. Even when France had surrendered, Hitler preferred to wait. The speed of the German advance meant that his armies needed to consolidate their positions; similarly the Luftwaffe had to establish new air bases before another major attack could be considered, even though Göring promised that his pilots could demolish the RAF whenever he gave the word. Besides, Hitler still hoped that the invasion would be unnecessary. Angered by Churchill's defiance, he nevertheless chose to believe that the British people were intimidated by German power and victories in Europe, and would soon eject their Prime Minister and sue for peace.

Hitler began to realize his mistake at the beginning of July. The British had been given every chance to negotiate peace; but diplomatic measures, secret approaches, broadcast speeches and even threats had failed to induce them to do his will. On 2 July, according to Wilhelm Keitel, his chief of staff, Hitler decided than an invasion was feasible 'providing that air superiority can be attained'. He issued orders for the provisional invasion plans, Operation *Seelöwe* (Sealion), to be updated and brought to readiness. And then on 3 July, at the Algerian port of Mers-el-Kebir, the Royal Navy destroyed the French fleet to prevent it falling into German hands — Churchill, in fact, had authorized the bombing of his own ally's fleet! Yet still the British public rallied round him! Infuriated into action, Hitler demanded to know in detail how the plans for Sealion were progressing.

Göring had already issued, on 30 June, his general orders for the preliminary air offensive. The Luftwaffe would launch a three-pronged assault, codenamed *Adlerangriff* (Eagle-attack), involving Luftflottes 2, 3 and 5, headed respectively by Kesselring, Sperrle and Stumpff. The assault would begin on *Adlertag*, Eagle-day, which would be any day that Hitler chose. Göring was so confident of success that he predicted the RAF

would be wiped out within two or three weeks.

Admiral Raeder and General Halder, for the Kriegsmarine and the Wehrmacht, were not so confident; nor were they entirely in agreement with each other. Halder envisaged 250,000 troops landing on a 100-mile front along England's southern coast. Raeder favoured a smaller force, 160,000 strong, being landed on a much narrower front between Eastbourne and Dover. A compromise was gradually forged, based on Raeder's plans. Both men agreed on one thing, however. The key to success lay in Luftwaffe hands.

On 16 July Hitler issued his Directive No. 16: 'Since England, in spite of her hopeless military situation, shows no sign of being ready to come to terms,' he proclaimed, 'I have decided to prepare a landing operation.' But first, he went on, 'The English air force must be so disabled in spirit and in fact that it cannot deliver any significant attack on the German crossing.'

Meanwhile the Luftwaffe pilots were deployed to new air bases in a wide crescent ringing southern England. Many were in high spirits after the Blitzkrieg success, greeting old comrades joyously as German POWs were released from the occupied countries. Others, who had encountered the cream of the RAF over Dunkirk or the Channel, waited more soberly for the great *Adlerangriff*. An uneasy feeling began to spread that Göring's predictions had been over-optimistic.

Operation Sealion

A seaborne invasion of Britain had first been mooted in October 1939 by Admiral Raeder, whose speculative initial plan was codenamed *Löwe* (Lion). *Seelöwe* (Sealion) was the more focused plan dating from late May 1940. It was intended to be a co-ordinated assault, the Kriegsmarine delivering the Wehrmacht across the Channel — but only when the Luftwaffe could guarantee air supremacy.

Although it underwent several modifications, Sealion's objective was to land 160,000 troops on a forty-mile coastal stretch of southeast England. This represented an early compromise between the army planners, who wanted a much larger force, and the navy, who knew that surprise depended on a more concentrated landing area. The troops would be transported in barges, fishing boats and tugs, guided by naval vessels along a narrow corridor across the Channel, both sides mined and guarded by submarines. Embarkation points would stretch from Rotterdam to Le Havre, and overall command would rest with Gerd von Rundstedt, promoted to *Feldmarschall* on 19 July.

Subsidiary operations included a deception plan, suggesting that the landings would be in northeast England, and preliminary arrangements for a military government in occupied Britain.

Wehrmacht advances

German Army proposal for Seelöwe

German Navy proposal for Seelöwe

Wehrmacht advances

U – boats

Mine-swept channel

U – boats to hold off the Royal Navy

The Line-Up

Just as the dates of the Battle of Britain are debatable, so the line-up of the two sides can never be accurately identified. The RAF officially dates the Battle as starting on 10 July 1940; but this is rejected by many historians who point out that the first major Luftwaffe attack did not come until mid-August. The dispositions of both RAF and Luftwaffe are even more difficult to pinpoint with precision, because log-books and other records were understandably neglected in the confusion of the times — and simply because so many were destroyed.

A definitive order of battle, therefore, is difficult to obtain. What this map shows is a generally agreed assessment of the opposing sides' positions in late July, when the German raids began to increase in intensity.

Numbers

Forces available to the Luftwaffe for operations against Britain at 10 August 1940:

Luftflotten 2 and 3	Total	Operational
Bombers (He.111, Ju.88, Do.17)	1,233	875
Dive bombers (Ju.87)	406	316
Fighters (Bf.109)	813	702
Fighter-bombers (Bf.110)	282	227
Long-range reconnaissance	65	45
Luftflotte 5		
Bombers (He.111, Ju.88, Do.17)	138	123
Fighter-bombers (Bf.110)	37	34
Long-range reconnaissance	48	33

Forces available to RAF Fighter Squadrons at 10 August 1940:

No. 10 Group (Southwest England and Wales)	Total	Operational
Spitfires	63	42
Hurricanes	50	37
Blenheims	16	11
No. 11 Group (South and Southeastern England)		
Spitfires	96	70
Hurricanes	216	165
Blenheims	36	20
No. 12 Group (Midlands and East Anglia)		
Spitfires	61	41
Hurricanes	51	37
Blenheims	26	17
Defiants	16	12
No. 13 Group (Northern England and Scotland)		
Spitfires	75	55
Hurricanes	149	111
Blenheims	15	10
Defiants	12	8
Gladiators	14	8
Fulmars	12	6

Fighter Command

Air Officer Commanding-in-Chief: Air Chief Marshal Sir Hugh Dowding. HQ: Bentley Priory, Stanmore, Middlesex.

Under Dowding's command came four fighter groups:

No. 10 Group under Air Officer Commanding: Air Vice-Marshal Sir Quintin Brand. No. 10 Group controlled squadrons based in southwest England and Wales.

No. 11 Group under Air Officer Commanding: Air Vice-Marshal Keith Park. No. 11 Group controlled squadrons based in the south and southeast of England which bore the brunt of the fighting.

No. 12 Group under Air Officer Commanding: Air Vice-Marshal Trafford Leigh-Mallory. No. 12 Group controlled squadrons based in the Midlands and East Anglia.

No. 13 Group under Air Officer Commanding: Air Vice-Marshal Richard Saul. No. 13 Group controlled squadrons in northern England and Scotland.

The Luftwaffe

Luftflotte 2 under Generalfeldmarschall Albert Kesselring. Luftflotte 2 controlled all air operations, bomber and fighter, based in northern France, Belgium and Holland. Its HQ was in Brussels. Under command of Luftflotte 2 were the following units, each of which controlled the Gruppe and Staffel:

I Fliegerkorps under Generaloberst Ulrich Grauert, based at Beauvais. Bombers — KG1 and KG76. Reconnaissance — 5/Aufklgr.122 and 4/Aufklgr.123.

II Fliegerkorps under General Bruno Lörzer, based at Ghent. Bombers — KG2, KG3, KG53. Stukas — II/Stg.1 and IV(Stuka) Gruppe LG1. Fighter-bombers — Erprobungsgruppe 210 and II/LG2.

IX Fliegerdivision under Generalmajor Joachim Coeler, based at Soesterberg. Bombers — KG4, KGr100, KG40, KGr126, Küflgr.106 and Aufklgr.122.

Jagdfliegerführer 2 under Generalmajor Theodor Osterkamp, based at Wissant. Fighters — JG3, JG26, JG51, JG52, JG54, I/LG2, ZG26 and ZG76.

Luftflotte 5 under Generaloberst Hans-Jurgen Stumpff, based at Stavanger, Norway. Controlled units in Scandinavia.

X Fliegerkorps under General-leutnant Hans Geisler, based at Stavanger. Bombers — KG26 and KG30. Long-range fighters — ZG76. Short-range fighters — JG77 (could not reach England). Reconnaissance — Küflgr.506, 1/Aufklgr.120, 1/Aufklgr.121, Aufklgr. Ob.d.L., and Aufklgr.22.

Luftflotte 3 under General-feldmarschall Hugo von Sperrle, based at Paris. Controlled units in northwest France.

IV Fliegerkorps under General Kurt Pflugbeil, based at Dinard. Bombers — LG1, KG27, Stg.3, KGr.806, 3/Aufklgr.31.

V Fliegerkorps under Generalleutnant Robert Ritter von Greim, based at Villa-coublay. Bombers — KG51, KG54, KG55.

VIII Fliegerkorps under Generalmajor Wolfram Freiherr von Richthofen, based at Deauville. Stukas — Stg.1, Stg.2, Stg.77, V/(Z)LG1. Reconnaissance — II/LG2, 2/Aufklgr.11 and 2/Aufklgr.123.

Jagdfliegerführer 3 under Oberst Werner Junck, based at Cherbourg. JG2, JG27, JG53 and ZG/2.

Luftflotte 5

Luftflotte 2

Luftflotte 3

RAF Bases	Luftwaffe Bases
■ Fighter Command H.Q.	● Bf. 109's
□ Group H.Q.	○ Stukas
⊙ Sector Stations	▼ Bf. 110's
○ Satellite Stations	▲ Twin Engined Bombers
+ Home Chain Low Radar	✕ Bombers and Bf. 110's
+ Home Chain Radar	+ Radar Station

Skirmishes

Before the Battle itself began, there was a series of isolated skirmishes over the Channel and around Britain's coasts. Already settled in at their new bases by late June, some of the Luftwaffe fighter pilots could not resist whooping across the water like over-enthusiastic cowboys.

Dowding did not take the bait. He wanted to preserve his fighters for the real battle ahead. The Luftwaffe fighters could do little harm, save to other fighters; they could even be welcomed as a chance for radar operators and Observer Corps spotters to improve their ability to estimate height and numbers. But sporadic interceptions resulted sometimes in loss on one side or the other. Small-scale nightly visits,

testing the defences or sowing mines outside ports, gave coastal batteries regular target practice. Long-range bombers like the Heinkel He.111s, armed with cameras, attempted to carry out photo-reconnaissance. But, as far as possible, Dowding held his fire.

By early July Dowding's 'chicks' were recovering their strength and Fighter Command was fast reforming. He was well aware of the menacing crescent of Luftwaffe bases curving from Norway round to northern France; the whole of Britain was now within range of German bombers. The small-scale raids were increasing in frequency and strength, often by day, targeting ports, military bases and industrial areas. On 4 July a single raid by thirty-three Stukas on Portland naval base resulted in 176 British seamen losing their lives. The enemy was testing him, but still Dowding held back. He knew the moment was coming when Göring's much-vaunted Luftwaffe would finally be unleashed.

The Luftwaffe, in fact, had begun an air blockade of Britain. While invasion plans were being refined, Hitler loosed his fighters on coastal and shipping targets, especially the Channel ports and convoys. Soon after midday on 10 July, a large raiding party formed up over the Pas de Calais: seventy aircraft in all, mainly Dornier bombers with an escort of Bf.109s and 110s. Minutes later they were heading for a westbound convoy that had been reported off Beachy Head, evidently hoping to escape notice in the drizzly conditions. But the raiders were met by a patrolling flight of six Hurricanes from 32 Squadron, Biggin Hill, which despite the huge disparity in numbers promptly waded in to the attack, soon backed up by sections of 56, 64, 74 and 111 Squadrons.

The ensuing mêlée was half hidden from observers in the convoy by the low cloud and falling bombs. What happened was that the Messerschmitt Bf.110s, the élite *Zerstörers* ('destroyers'), suddenly found themselves outclassed. Despite their formidable forward firepower, they were no match for the highly manoeuvrable Hurricanes, which they kept at bay only by forming into a defensive circle like wagon trains in the Wild West. Defence of the Dornier bombers now depended solely on the Bf.109s. When the air cleared, the British had lost one ship and three Hurricanes, but four 109s had been shot down.

The Luftwaffe made other raids that day, at Falmouth, Swansea and elsewhere; in all they killed thirty civilians. At the end of the day the RAF had flown 610 sorties and lost six fighters — but the Luftwaffe had lost a total of thirteen aircraft. It had been the first major confrontation of the Germans' so-called *Kanalkampf* ('Channel battle'), and the first day of the Battle of Britain.

Coastal Convoy Routes 1940

Luftwaffe attacks, July/August 1940

Kanalkampf

For British historians, the Battle of Britain officially ran from 10 July to 31 October. German historians hold that the battle didn't begin until 13 August 1940 — *Adlertag* — although considerable air action took place before and after these dates.

Hitler, still hoping to negotiate an end to the war, forbade attacks against civilian targets, especially London, but sanctioned Luftwaffe action against shipping and ports, seeing it as an extension of the U-boat blockade against Britain's supply routes. Although the invasion plans were incomplete, such action would also weaken the defence. Although sporadic attacks still took place on inland targets, the coastal raids became known to Luftwaffe aircrew as the *Kanalkampf* — the Channel War.

10 July. Raid of 70 plus on coastal convoy off Dover. RAF losses: 6. Luftwaffe losses: 13.

11 July. Raids of 30 plus and two of 24 plus on convoys off the east and south coasts; Portland, Portsmouth and other harbours raided. During the Portland attack a Bf.110 crashes, killing Göring's nephew. RAF losses: 4. Luftwaffe losses: 20.

12 July. Raids on east and south coast shipping, heavy night raid on Bristol and south Wales. RAF losses: 6. Luftwaffe losses: 7.

13 July. Fog reduces activity: shipping attacked off Dover and Portland. RAF losses: 1. Luftwaffe losses: 7.

14 July. Raids on shipping off Dover and the Dorset coast. RAF losses: 4. Luftwaffe losses: 2.

15 July. Low cloud and rain, but shipping is attacked in Thames estuary. RAF losses: 1. Luftwaffe losses: 3.

16 July. Fog limits activity, but several Luftwaffe airmen pay for their persistence with their lives. RAF losses: 2. Luftwaffe losses: 3.

17 July. Rainy weather clears to allow small-scale operations against shipping off Scotland and the east coast. Only 250 RAF sorties flown. RAF loss: 1. Luftwaffe losses: 2.

18 July. Weather hinders Luftwaffe action. Raids against south and east coast shipping. Goodwin lightship sunk. RAF losses: 2. Luftwaffe losses: 4.

19 July. Fair, if showery, weather leads to increased activity. RAF flies over 700 sorties and loses the exchange. Six out of nine 141 Squadron Defiants from Hawkinge shot down by Bf.109s in morning. Heavy raid on Dover in afternoon. RAF losses: 8. Luftwaffe losses: 2. Figures prompt Hitler to make his 'last appeal to reason' speech to Reichstag.

Convoy

Just as Göring's 'eagles' hoped, the constant round of dogfights began to tell on the weary pilots of Fighter Command. German tactics were still to blockade British ports by air attacks and minelaying and to harass all shipping. Dover harbour was raided so often that it earned the name of 'Hellfire Corner'. The Channel continued to be the focus of activity, but raids were made on Glasgow and the Firth of Forth, Liverpool and Hull, Bristol and Ipswich. And every time the raiders came, the RAF had to scramble.

Fighter Command's workload increased sharply during the beginning of July and reached a level comparable with that needed to cover the Dunkirk evacuation. On just one day, 8 July, 300 sorties were flown over shipping.

Convoys were coming in for terrible punishment. Despite the combined efforts of the Royal Navy and Fighter Command, it was inevitable that some bombs should get through. In fact, on 27 July two destroyers were hit and sunk, and a third damaged, during a raid on Convoy Bacon off Harwich. The Navy withdrew, leaving convoy protection entirely to Dowding's slender resources.

But still they continued: Snail, Agent, Cable, Bosom and all the other strangely named convoys. Despite the risk from mines, despite the constant attentions of the Luftwaffe, despite the fact that most cargoes could perfectly well go by rail, shipping activities gave a visible sign that Britain was still functioning as normal — albeit with Fighter Command overhead.

The pattern of daily raids on shipping and harbours was broken only by adverse weather conditions: fog, thunderstorms, so much rain that airfields on both sides of the Channel were

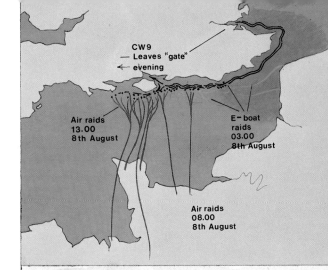

CW9
— Leaves "gate"
← evening

Air raids
13.00
8th August

E-boat
raids
03.00
8th August

Air raids
08.00
8th August

waterlogged for a time. By the end of July the RAF had flown more than 10,000 sorties and a total of nearly 200 raiders had been shot down since the Battle began, for the loss of around seventy aircraft. Production was in full swing now, and Dowding's fighters were quickly replaced from the factory lines or repair units; but he was down to 1,434 pilots, and he well knew the battle proper had yet to begin.

Even so, those weary young men in their Spitfires and Hurricanes could not ignore the desperate plight of merchant seamen in convoys. The colliers or 'coalscuttle brigade' were a regular target. Hugging the coast they would chug from port to port, hoping to escape attention but usually in vain. Often it was the Stukas that shrieked out of the mist to deposit a tower of water where its bomb near-missed the boat. Then the gallant defenders arrived. The crackle of gunfire, the roar of engines filled the air. Sometimes an aircraft would descend in a last fatal dive; sometimes a parachute floated down to the sea. But sometimes the bomb hit its target.

At the end of July, convoys were ordered to move only by night. Although deep in preparations for Göring's *Adlerangriff*, the Luftwaffe's harassment of convoys did not falter. In the early hours of 8 August, one particular convoy found that even the night offered no protection. Convoy Peewit was off the Kent coast when an enemy radar unit, recently set up on a clifftop position south of Calais, spotted it through the darkness. Guided by their radar information, the Germans now made a determined effort to sink the convoy, using bombers and fighters by day and E-boats by night, pursuing the surviving ships westwards as they fled for safety off the Isle of Wight. For three days the attacks went on, repulsed by the RAF, resuming again later. Casualties were heavy on both sides. Most of the ships were sunk. The Luftwaffe lost a total of thirty-one aircraft, the RAF twenty. All coastal convoys were suspended for the foreseeable future.

Peewit

A large convoy of westbound ships, Convoy CW9 or 'Peewit', assembled in the Thames Estuary before making a night sailing on 7 August. Rounding the Kent coast in the dark early morning of the 8th, the convoy was spotted by enemy radar. The Germans had built a radar installation at Wissant, which now triggered an attack on the convoy. Despite intervention by the RAF, by dawn on the 8th three ships had been sunk. The survivors scattered, then ploughed gamely on, leaving the rescue ships to take a battering; some of them were also sunk. That same afternoon the raiders returned to attack the convoy again and another eight ships were sunk. Day and night the battering continued. In the end, just 4 out of the 20 ships arrived safely at Swanage.

Unavailing Defiants

Long before convoy operations were halted, Fighter Command had begun to reassess tactics and procedure. Like the Luftwaffe 'eagles', the RAF had already learnt painful lessons from these opening days of the Battle. Experienced men like Alan Deere and Peter Townsend, who would contribute in no small part to the ultimate victory, suffered narrow escapes during this period. Al Deere, the New Zealander, collided with a Messerschmitt and only just managed a wheels-up landing back at Manston, while Peter Townsend's Hurricane caught a flurry of gunfire from a Do.17 and he was forced to bale out; he parachuted into the sea off Harwich, landed in a minefield, was rescued by fishermen, plied with rum and made it back to his base at Debden in time to fly another sortie — relatively sober — that same evening.

One lesson the RAF had learnt was not to place too much reliance on radar. Radar was a precious ally, but it was no panacea. It required skilful interpretation; sometimes the operators misread the echoes on their screen, underestimating the number of raiders or their altitude. As a result, the controllers would send up too few fighters or direct them to the wrong place. Besides, radar was not yet available for air-to-air use; Dowding's pilots still depended on visual sightings to find their foe. And, though the myth persists that the Battle of Britain was fought in clear blue skies, many of the clashes of these first few weeks were confused encounters amid cloud and squalls of rain.

Secondly, as Dowding well knew, though his fighters were doling out more punishment than they took, the aircraft they shot down were — in accordance with orders — mainly bombers. The

Bf.109s learnt to attack Defiants from their blind-spots: from ahead or below. Hence their success against 141 Squadron on 19 July.

enemy fighters too often survived to return another day. While flights of Hurricanes and Spitfires repulsed packs of twenty or thirty bombers, attacking a convoy perhaps or Dover harbour again, they were frequently bounced from above by the Messerschmitt fighters, Bf.109s. Once the 109s joined in it was every man for himself; the bombers were, of necessity, forgotten. The lesson was clear. The Spitfires and particularly the Hurricanes would have to increase their high-altitude performance to match the 109s. Already the de Havilland variable-pitch propeller was being fitted to existing aircraft, while an even more advanced propeller, the Rotol constant-speed, variable-pitch airscrew, underwent final tests. And, since the Spitfire's rate of climb and speed at altitude was slightly superior, henceforth the Spitfire would focus more on enemy fighters while the Hurricane took on the bombers.

Thirdly, the front-line defenders, outnumbered though they were, would not in future include

Defiants; nor would the Blenheim fighters make much further contribution, except in the hours of darkness.

At the start of the Battle, Fighter Command included two squadrons of Defiants and six of Blenheims. Both types of aircraft had acquitted themselves well over France and Dunkirk; the Defiants alone notched up over sixty 'kills' by the end of May, mostly bombers. But the Defiant was some 40mph slower than the Messerschmitts, the Blenheim about 80mph slower, and both were easily outgunned by the German fighters. The Blenheim was used mainly against the enemy bombers, but on 19 July a flight of nine Defiants from 141 Squadron was thrown alone into the front line, like sacrificial lambs.

The Defiants took off from Hawkinge, near Folkestone, in the early afternoon, to patrol the Kent coast and provide air cover for a passing convoy. The Bf.109s came out of nowhere. There was no warning from the controllers. Twenty 109s swooped out of the sky and picked off the Defiants like ducks in a shooting gallery. Minutes later, five had fallen into the sea. Another crash-landed at Hawkinge. The remaining three were rescued by Hurricanes from 111 Squadron; but 141 Squadron had been decimated. The remainder of the squadron was despatched to Scotland's Turnhouse sector, to recuperate its losses and henceforth to tackle bombers only at night.

The Defiants and Blenheims having withdrawn, Dowding's front-line defence was growing thinner by the day. And the moment of truth was approaching.

141 Squadron's Defiants were withdrawn from the Battle within days of joining it in July. A similar fate later met 264 Squadron, which lost all but three of its Defiants within a week.

The Bottom Line

Apart from lack of performance, the Defiant's main fault was that its armament was mounted in a turret which had a restricted field of fire: it couldn't fire below or ahead. The gunner also required a steady flying platform from which to aim — unlikely in a dogfight. Over Dunkirk, the Luftwaffe used the classic diving attack from the rear on a squadron of 'Hurricanes', only to be met by the fire from forty-eight machine guns.

The Blenheim F.1, fighter version of a bomber design, was also no match for Bf.109s but later made a useful stop-gap night fighter.

Boulton Paul Defiant
A single-engined monoplane fighter, with two-man crew. **Engine:** Rolls-Royce Merlin III V-12 cylinder in line, 1030hp. **Dimensions:** Span 39' 4" (11.99m). Length 35' 4" (10.77m). Height 12' 2" (3.71m). Wing area 250sq.ft. (23.23sq.m.). **Weight:** empty 6282lb (2852kg), loaded 7110lb (3228kg). **Performance:** Top speed 304mph (489kph) at 16,500ft (5029m). Cruise speed 240mph (386kph). Rate of climb 2120ft/min (646m/min). Time to 18,000ft (5486m) 10.2 min. Ceiling 30,200ft (9205m). Range 600 miles (966km). **Armament:** Four .303" (7.7mm) Browning machine guns in power turret.

Bristol Blenheim IF
A twin-engined monoplane fighter with two- or three-man crew. **Engines:** Two Bristol Mercury XV 9-cylinder radials, 920hp. **Dimensions:** Span 56' 4" (17.17m). Length 42' 7" (12.98m). Height 10' 0" (3.05m). Wing area 469sq.ft. (43.65 sq.m.). **Weight:** empty 9200lb (4177kg), loaded 14,500lb (6583kg). **Performance:** Top speed 260mph (418kph) at 12,000ft (3658m). Cruise speed 200mph (322kph). Rate of climb 1540ft/min (469m/min). Ceiling 24,600ft (7498m). Range 1460 miles (2350km). **Armament:** Four .303" (7.7mm) Browning machine guns in under-fuselage pack and one or two .303" Vickers K machine guns in turret.

Adlertag

On 1 August 1940, Hitler issued Directive No. 17 for 'the final conquest of England'. The Luftwaffe would, he ordered, 'overpower the English air force ... in the shortest possible time'. Göring's pilots were to concentrate their attacks on the RAF itself — its aircraft, airfields, base installations and communications — and on the aircraft industry; as yet civilian targets were to be avoided. When air superiority had been achieved the Luftwaffe could continue to raid British ports and shipping, but with one proviso: 'Attacks on south coast ports will be made on the smallest possible scale in view of our own forthcoming operations.' The *Kanalkampf* was over and the *Adlerangriff* was about to begin — 'on or after 5 August', Hitler directed, leaving the Luftwaffe chief to make the final choice of *Adlertag*, 'Eagle Day'.

Throughout the past weeks, reclining in the luxury of his special train at Le Coudray, Göring had remained blithely confident, despite the rising toll inflicted on his pilots by RAF fighters. Some of his senior officers and staff were not so sure. The Luftwaffe's strength lay in Blitzkrieg tactics, spearheading a joint air–ground attack; moreover, the RAF had already proved itself a redoubtable adversary. Their qualms would have deepened if they had known that Luftwaffe intelligence had seriously underestimated British radar capabilities and failed to identify any of the RAF's group or sector headquarters. And of course the German Enigma coding system had been broken; although Dowding was not yet in on the Ultra secret, he was by now starting to receive advance information about some of the German plans.

On 6 August Göring summoned his Luftflotte commanders to Karinhall, his estate forty miles from Berlin. *Adlertag*, he told them, would be 10 August. The meteorologists predicted a spell of fine weather to begin on the 10th, a propitious augury for the outcome of the battle. Brushing aside all doubts expressed by Kesselring and Sperrle, he led them on a tour of his art collection, then sent them off to make final preparations.

On the 8th, as we have seen, the Luftwaffe took heavy casualties, mainly as a result of its attacks on Convoy Peewit — but it was not these losses so much as unsettled weather that caused the postponement of *Adlertag* on the 9th: the forecasters had been wrong. The great air assault would now commence on 13 August. Meanwhile preliminary attacks were made on naval and air bases along the south coast and on radar stations. In fact, 11–12 August saw the heaviest fighting of the battle so far: on the 11th the Luftwaffe lost thirty-eight aircraft and the RAF thirty-two, on the 12th the figures were thirty-one and twenty-two respectively. Five radar stations were damaged, most seriously the one at Ventnor, on the Isle of Wight, which was attacked by a total of fifteen Ju.88s. But even Ventnor was functioning again within three days.

Simultaneously Göring's pilots turned their deadly attentions on RAF stations like Manston, Lympne and Hawkinge, in order to annihilate the opposition's front-line bases, and on major industrial targets like the Spitfire factory at Woolston, Southampton. Their success was mixed, but the German commanders were sufficiently encouraged to let the morrow's plans stand.

At 0500 hours on 13 August the first bombers took off from their airfields in northeast France. Seventy-four Dorniers of KG2 set off towards the Thames Estuary with Oberst Johannes Fink in the lead. All seemed well as they crossed the French coast and their fighter escort of Bf.110s from ZG26 appeared and joined them, but after a remarkable show of aerobatics the escort flew off, leaving the bombers alone. Oberst Fink and his formation carried on, not knowing that Göring had postponed operations due to a forecast of bad weather. What the Bf.110 pilots had been trying to do was to turn back the Dorniers as best they could; because the bombers were on different radio frequencies they could not be contacted directly. KG2 lost five Dorniers in their lone attack, but they were not the only unit that did not receive instructions to cancel operations. Even three hours later the Bf.110 crews of I/ZG26 had not had their orders cancelled and they set off to find the bombers they were to escort.

It was not until 1530 hours that the real attack began and was picked up by radar stations in the West Country as the intruders headed for the Solent, Hampshire and Dorset. 120 Ju.88s, 30 Bf.110s, 90 Ju.87s and 60 Bf.109s were met by fighters from 10 Group, and heavy losses were sustained by the Bf.110 and Stuka units as the escort fighters turned back when short of fuel. In the southeast the most successful attack was made by Stukas of LG1 which attacked Detling Airfield and temporarily put it out of action. The day had cost the Luftwaffe twenty-nine aircraft; the RAF lost fourteen fighters, but only three of the pilots were killed.

Base Intentions

Adlertag had merely raised the curtain on the drama of the next three weeks. The new intensity of Luftwaffe attacks was obvious to everyone in southern Britain. Day after day, the sirens wailed over city and town, naval base and airfield, warning of yet another huge raid to come. Sixty or eighty Dorniers, perhaps, from Cambrai and Arras; or longer-range bombers like the Heinkel 111s and Junkers 88s from bases in the Netherlands. But Fighter Command put up a determined defence, aided by the advance warning provided by radar and the ever-vigilant controllers.

The radar operators would watch, on their glowing cathode-ray screens, the flickering traces that indicated a massive swarm assembling over the Cherbourg peninsula or the Pas de Calais. Coolly they would assess the numbers involved, then alert the controllers, advising them of the

raiders' course when they finally headed for Britain. But it was like a game of chess, a sophisticated battle of wits on a giant scale, the controllers trying to guess the enemy's targets and the Luftwaffe fighter pilots trying to lure Dowding's fighters away from the bombers.

The controllers soon became adept at scrambling RAF fighters at just the right moment: not too early, or they might run out of fuel and have to return to base; nor too late, or they might still be climbing into the air when the enemy arrived. But the Germans were learning too. Deadly games of bluff and counter-bluff developed as the Luftwaffe chiefs sought to outwit their opponents, and sometimes they succeeded. On one occasion a slow-flying formation led the controllers to anticipate a bomber raid; but when the RAF fighters made the interception they found a large force of Messerschmitt fighters flying at bomber speed.

A general pattern was discernible in this new spate of attacks: the enemy's intention was to demolish RAF airbases, particularly in southern England. Repeated mass attacks were made on Manston, Lympne, Middle Wallop, Croydon and other bases. On 18 August, for example, fifty Do.17s and another fifty Ju.88s, flying at an altitude of 17,000ft (5182m), seemed to be making for Biggin Hill or Kenley; but as the RAF fighters scrambled to meet them they realized, too late, that they had been duped. Far below, screaming in at tree-top level, eight Dorniers made a swift and savage attack on Kenley's ground installations. The airfield defences put up a tremendous barrage, however, combining AA fire with PAC (parachute and cable) launchers; these rocket-propelled wires flew into the air then hung there on small parachutes before drifting slowly back to earth. The dangling cables caught at least one low-flying Dornier at Kenley, and with the help of a shell hit brought it to the ground.

The gloves were off now. Grimly determined adversaries met in the skies like duellists. One ploy met another; feint matched feint. Sometimes a desperate Hurricane or Spitfire pilot flew head-on towards an intruder, guns spewing fire at the enemy aircrew huddled in their glazed cockpit, in an attempt to break the German pilot's nerve; inevitably there were occasional hideous collisions. Often the Bf.109s, stacked up to nearly 30,000ft (9144m), would bounce the RAF fighters and a violent dogfight would ensue. Wheeling, ducking, firing, turning, straining machines and men would swoop through the air in every direction; then suddenly one would be gone, diving earthwards, while the survivors nursed their aircraft back to base. Dowding's pilots had a slight advantage here; they were usually within gliding distance of an RAF base, and some made remarkable landings despite bullet-riddled, mutilated aircraft.

The German pilots faced a longer homeward flight, with the Channel as an extra hurdle. If, that is, they survived the dogfights — for the RAF was continuing to hold the upper hand.

Into August

Despite the myth that the Battle of Britain was fought in clear, sun-drenched skies, the weather during the summer of 1940 was not good. Fortunately the cloud and rain often concealed exposed channel shipping and coastal towns from attack. This pattern continued throughout July and into August, with the Straits and town of Dover particularly hard hit.

20 July. Shipping dive-bombed and Dover again attacked between thunderstorms. RAF losses: 3. Luftwaffe losses: 9.

21–26 July. Channel convoys and other shipping attacked. An escort destroyer damaged. RAF losses: 19. Luftwaffe losses: 37.

27 July. Two destroyers sunk and two damaged in raids on convoys in the Straits of Dover harbour. Navy withdraws destroyers. Fighter Command now has 28 squadrons in southeast Britain but flies only 496 sorties. RAF loss: 1. Luftwaffe losses: 4.

28–31 July. Unsettled and often poor weather continues. When fine, raids continue against shipping and ports round the southwest, southern and eastern British coast, with Dover and the Straits getting more than their fair share. RAF losses over the period: 11. Luftwaffe: 31, including an He.59 rescue seaplane bearing civil markings, but escorted by Bf.109s. Pilots ordered to attack them as suspected spy-planes.

1 August. The pattern continues. A night raid on the West Country scatters Hitler's 'Last Appeal to Reason' leaflets over empty countryside. RAF losses: 2. Luftwaffe losses: 5.

2–7 August. Alternating days of good and bad weather see Luftwaffe activity decline. Fighter Command flies between 390 and 480 sorties per day, weather permitting. Britain prepares for expected invasion, but doesn't realize that the reduced Luftwaffe activity is to prepare for *Adlerangriff*, the 'Eagles' Attack', initially planned for 10 August. RAF loss: 1. Luftwaffe losses: 14.

8 August. Three large-scale attacks by Stukas launched against convoy 'Peewit'.

9–10 August. A quiet time with little activity. *Adlerangriff* postponed due to bad weather. RAF losses: 4. Luftwaffe losses: 5.

11 August. 150 bombers escorted by fighters attack the naval docks of Portland, Dorset, while a diversionary raid makes for Dover. It is a heavy and confusing day's fighting. RAF losses: 32. Luftwaffe losses: 38.

12 August. Anticipating the new *Adlertag* on 13 August, the Luftwaffe strikes channel convoys and Portsmouth harbour, but more importantly at Chain Home radar stations along the south coast and installations at Ventnor, Isle of Wight. Lympne and Hawkinge RAF stations are hit and Manston has its first raid, but all are quickly back in action. Fighter Command flies 732 sorties. RAF losses: 22. Luftwaffe losses: 31

The Ides of August

On 15 August, the fine weather that Göring's meteorologists had been predicting finally arrived. Now the Luftwaffe could really flex its muscles. In these clear skies, the bomber escorts would see trouble well in advance and be able to meet it; the bombers would have no difficulty finding their targets. An immediate 'knock-out attack' was launched. So far only Luftflotten 2 and 3 had been involved; now Luftflotte 5, based in Scandinavia, would also be unleashed.

But the Luftwaffe planners unwittingly laid their plans on faulty premises. German intelligence had consistently underestimated the numbers of RAF fighter aircraft and assumed that all Dowding's Spitfires and Hurricanes were based in the south of the country. The north, it was thought, lacked any significant fighter cover while the RAF struggled to meet the assault from across the Channel.

The Luftwaffe were relying on information prepared by Oberleutnant Josef Schmid for his 'Studie Blau' issued on 16 July 1940. Subsequent reconnaissance sorties added detail to the report but this was also wrongly interpreted. For instance, the airfields at Upavon, Worthy Down and Eastchurch were reported to be operational fighter stations, but

in reality they were training and Coastal Command bases. What were taken as Hurricanes and Hawker Demon biplanes at Lee-on-Solent and Detling were actually Skuas and Swordfish belonging to the Fleet Air Arm. Such errors would not have been serious had future attacks not been based on this intelligence. For great effort was expended in attacking all of these targets in the early part of the Battle.

The same intelligence report included an estimate of the strength of Fighter Command. It was thought that there were fifty squadrons with a total of 900 aircraft, about 675 of which would be serviceable at any one time. Sixty per cent of these aircraft were thought to be Hurricanes and the remaining forty per cent Spitfires. These numbers were not too inaccurate; as British figures at the same time show, the RAF actually had 1052 aircraft with squadrons, 658 of which were operational. What was not realized, though, was that around 500 aircraft were being readied in storage units.

The 'eagles' of Generaloberst Stumpff's Luftflotte 5 were restless and eager for action. However, the pilots of Fighter Command's No. 12 and 13 Groups were equally impatient — like 72 and 79 Squadrons at Acklington and 616 Squadron at Leconfield. Many of them had been sent north to recuperate after the Continental battles, but now they felt excluded from

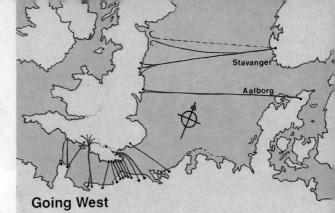

the action. They would, however, see plenty on this day.

The first raids were, as usual, in the south. Huge formations of 100 or more bombers rumbled across the Channel, arriving over Kent at about 1100 hours: Dorniers, Heinkels, Junkers 88s and 87s, escorted by Bf.109s and 110s. Their targets, again, were Dover and the airfields; once more Hawkinge and Lympne took a drubbing. Further raids would develop during the afternoon and evening, stepping up the pressure on the squadrons of No. 11 and 10 Groups. Martlesham Heath, Lympne again, Manston, West Malling, Middle Wallop, Biggin Hill; aircraft and engine factories at Rochester; radar stations at Dover, Bawdsey and Foreness; Portland Harbour, Deal and Folkestone. The raiders came in such concentration that every available Hurricane and Spitfire from 10 and 11 Groups was needed to thwart the attacks.

Meanwhile, soon after noon, the northeast controllers sounded the alert. Radar had picked up the approach of hostile aircraft over the North Sea. No. 13 Group's ops room at Watnall, near Nottingham, was suddenly buzzing with life. 'Scramble, scramble, scramble!' the controllers urged. The raiders were approaching Tyneside, assessments of their numbers growing by the minute. Forty-plus, fifty-plus... In fact there were sixty-five He.111s from *Kampfgeschwader* 26 in Stavanger, escorted by thirty-four Bf.110s from *Zerstörergeschwader* 76, specially fitted with auxiliary fuel tanks. Minutes later another hostile formation was reported down the coast: fifty unescorted Ju.88s from KG 30 in Aalborg, Denmark.

The German bombers had flown a nerve-racking ninety minutes or so across the featureless North Sea, their bombloads reduced to help extend their range, and the first wave made navigation errors that left them floundering before their attack even began. And they met a savage response from the defenders. Some of the bombers jettisoned their bombs and fled for home. Others pressed on through the angry, wheeling ranks of RAF fighters and managed to cause some minor damage in the Sunderland area. The second wave, the Ju.88s, made a few hits on Driffield and Bridlington before they too, harried by 616 and 73 Squadrons, turned for home.

When the skies had cleared and the defenders went back to base for lunch, eight He.111s were missing along with seven Bf.110s and seven Ju.88s. The RAF had suffered only one loss. Altogether the Luftwaffe flew over 2000 sorties on this day and lost sixty-three aircraft on operations against Britain. Fighter Command flew 974 sorties and lost thirty-five aircraft, with thirteen pilots killed, three taken prisoner in France, and sixteen injured.

The results trickling in to Karinhall, Göring's lavish estate, were dismissed at first as unbelievable. Eventually, however, even he had to face facts. He was furious. He blamed the pilots. He demanded that the Luftflotte commanders explain their failure. But in the end he had to acknowledge that the tactics he himself had approved would have to be completely reappraised.

Going West

Air Operations 15 August 1940

The weather forecast read well for the Luftwaffe commanders and finally the go-ahead was given for the maximum effort attack against the RAF and its airfields.

The first raid did not come until the late morning when 100 Stukas bombed Lympne and Hawkinge. In the early afternoon He.111 bombers escorted by Bf.110 long-range fighters attempted a surprise attack. The raid was first seen by radar off the Firth of Forth and plotted as it flew southwards towards Tynemouth. 13 Group Headquarters ordered 72 Squadron's Spitfires and 605 Squadron's Hurricanes to intercept with 79 and 607 Squadrons waiting in the wings. Squadron Leader Graham led 72 Squadron into an attack on 65 Heinkels of KG26 and 34 Bf.110s of I/ZG76. The Messerschmitts immediately went into a tail-chasing defensive circle while the bombers split into two forces heading to landfall and a few heading back to Norway. 607, 605, 41 and 79 Squadrons met the two persistent formations and turned them back before they could reach their targets. 8 Heinkels and 7 Bf.110s failed to return, but only a single Hurricane of 605 Squadron was lost.

At the same time 50 Ju.88s of KG30 were approaching No. 12 Group's air space. Hurricanes of 73 Squadron and Spitfires of 616 Squadron engaged the bombers, but could not stop them before they attacked the bomber station at Driffield, Yorkshire, where 10 Whitley heavy bombers were wrecked on the ground. 7 Ju.88s failed to return and 3 more were damaged; no RAF fighters were lost.

In the south of England a force of Ju.87s and Bf.110s escorted by Bf.109s attacked the relatively unimportant airfield of Martlesham Heath, Suffolk. At 1530 around 250 aircraft crossed the Kent coast and were engaged by seven fighter squadrons which caused the formation to scatter. Towards evening 250 aircraft crossed the Isle of Wight and attacked targets in Hampshire and Wiltshire, but were set upon by eleven fighter squadrons which brought down 25 raiders. Finally fighter-bombers swept in just before 1900 and bombed Croydon airfield.

Statistics of 'Adlertag': RAF claims 183 Luftwaffe aircraft destroyed; Luftwaffe claims 101 RAF aircraft destroyed. Actual losses: RAF — 35 aircraft (13 pilots killed and three taken prisoner); Luftwaffe — 63 aircraft and their crews lost in operations against Britain.

Manston

Already the Luftwaffe pilots had demonstrated that one of their favourite targets was Manston. It was close, just forty miles across the Channel from their own nearest bases in the Pas de Calais. And it was easy to find, lying at the neck of the Kent knob known as the Isle of Thanet. Manston therefore came in for particular attention — though other southeastern airfields came a close second. In the battle of the bases, Manston's experiences can perhaps be used to epitomize the constant and ferocious battering that marked out this stage of the Battle.

An airfield had been at Manston since 1916 and it was even at that time seen as a base for the defence of London. On 22 August 1917, a Gotha bomber intent on attacking the capital had been brought down and crashed close to the airfield.

An all-grass airfield, popular with squadron commanders who liked to get all their aircraft off the ground simultaneously, Manston belonged to Hornchurch D sector and was home base to the night-flying Blenheims of 600 (City of London) Squadron. A Spitfire squadron, No. 65, also used Manston as an occasional base though normally operating from Hornchurch. On 12 August, when the first major raid began, twelve Spitfires were just taking off when the Dorniers swept in from the sea. Five minutes later 150 HE bombs had blasted hangars and workshops, pitting the field with white craters and riming everything with chalk dust. Amazingly, only one of the Spitfires was slightly damaged; the rest clawed their way into the air to join the whirling dogfight between Messerschmitt escorts and other patrolling Spitfires.

Local Army units helped to fill the craters on Manston's pitted airfield and by dawn the following day it was fit for use again. Only hours later, however, the Luftwaffe returned: at lunchtime on the 13th, a *Staffel* of Bf.109s strafed the field. And the following day, again at lunchtime, several Bf.110s swept through in a sudden low-level attack; four more hangars were destroyed but the ground crew shot down one of the Messerschmitts and winged another.

By now the airfield was a crazy maze of ridges and craters. Pilots continued to take off and land, but it was luck more than judgement that saved their undercarriages. The ground crews were busier than ever, continuing to service the aircraft while labouring to fill the craters with crushed chalk, to clear up the workshops and to salvage whatever tools and spares had not been irretrievably damaged. On 15 August the Bf.109s came back. And on the 16th. The 18th. The 20th. The 22nd. The 24th. Manston was a complete shambles; it would surely have to close.

Manston was in fact *too* far forward. Aircraft taking off from its grassy field were forced to climb very steeply to meet the oncoming enemy, or risked being bounced by Luftwaffe fighters. In the base itself the constant strain on ground crew and administrative personnel began to tell, though rumours of snapped nerve and collapse were rapidly quashed. (Although never officially admitted, there is certainly evidence that at least some ground crews took fright in the midst of these air attacks and refused to come out of their underground shelters.) Adding to the confusion, 264 Squadron of Defiants was sent to Manston on 24 August; but, just as before, their gallant efforts met a crushing response and two days later the few survivors were withdrawn.

Long before now, questions had begun to be voiced about the value of such a base. Why put men through this ordeal? Why bother to repair the airfield? Why not close it down? The suspicion was that Manston stayed open only because closure would affect morale at home and signal defeat to the enemy. But on 26 August Churchill was touring Kent and happened to visit Manston. Horrified at the devastation, he made his views clear: Manston should close. Within days the base was evacuated. In future it would be used only as an emergency landing site.

Of the closure of the airfield the daily diary records only: 'Later it was decided to evacuate permanently all administrative personnel and those required in connection with station defence and servicing of aircraft. Accommodation for evacuated personnel was found in Westgate.'

It was, however, the only airfield that had to be abandoned during those raging days of August 1940.

The Daily Grind
Diary of RAF Manston

12 August. The airfield was bombed by 15 Bf.110s of the specialist fighter-bomber unit *Erprobungsgruppe 210* and 18 Do.17s of KG2. The attack came just as the Spitfires of 65 Squadron were taking off. 150 250kg bombs were dropped which completely gutted and destroyed the workshops. Two hangars were damaged and bomb craters put runways out of action for 24 hours. The returning German crews claimed that the airfield had been totally destroyed, but they had been misled by the huge clouds of smoke and dust which rose up from the airfield and obscured everything.

14 August. Reconnaissance proved the airfield to still be operational so once more 16 Bf.110 fighter-bombers of Erprobungsgruppe 210 were sent to attack. This time they damaged 4 hangars and destroyed 3 Blenheims belonging to 600 Squadron. The ground crews of 600 Squadron opened fire with a 20mm cannon which had been erected on a make-shift platform and shot one raider down while the Royal Artillery shot down another with a 40mm Bofors gun. About 50 bomb craters were made and were filled in within a few hours.

15 August. Bf.110s damaged the hangars again.

16 August. Bf.109s attacked and destroyed a Spitfire and a Blenheim on the ground.

18 August. Bf.109s made a surprise attack and there was no time for any warning to be given. The raid caught mechanics in the open as they were working on Spitfires of 266 Squadron which had flown down from Hornchurch. One man was killed and 15 injured. 2 Spitfires were destroyed, 6 more badly damaged.

20 August. Small attack, little damage.

22 August. Another small raid, but no casualties.

24 August. The worst attack of the battle. Defiants of 264 Squadron were caught on the ground refuelling when bombers attacked, but some managed to take off as the bombs fell. Of these, three were shot down by Bf.109s over the Channel and their crews killed; 2 other Defiants were severely damaged in the combat. 7 men on the ground were killed and many more injured. Bomb craters and unexploded bombs were found all over the airfield; aircraft and buildings caught fire. All non-essential personnel were evacuated. All communications were cut so no contact could be made with No. 11 Group HQ. A runner was sent on a bicycle to Maidstone to report news.

28 August. Winston Churchill made a visit to see the damage for himself. From this time Manston was used only as a forward base for fighters and for Lysanders helping with air–sea rescue work.

The Fatal Mistake

By the third week of August, leaders on both sides of the Channel knew that the climax of the Battle was approaching. On the 19th Göring was talking about 'the decisive period'. On the 20th, Churchill was standing up in the House of Commons and paying public tribute to Fighter Command: 'Never in the field of human conflict was so much owed by so many to so few.' But the worst was yet to come.

After several cloudy, showery days, 24 August dawned fine. The Luftwaffe took the opportunity for a burst of renewed activity. Manston was raided several times, along with Hornchurch and North Weald airfields. Ramsgate, Dover, Portsmouth and Southampton were heavily bombed. At Portsmouth some of the raiders missed the naval base and hit civilian targets instead: 117 lost their lives. Altogether the Luftwaffe lost thirty-eight aircraft, the RAF twenty-two.

Continuing their raids into the night, the German pilots headed for South Wales, Birmingham and Yorkshire, to wreak havoc on industrial targets.

Smaller raids were planned on southeast England, including one on the oil storage tanks at Thames Haven. But these bombers failed to spot their target. They swept towards London, dropping their bombs indiscriminately on the East End, the City and elsewhere. Nine people died on the ground.

Surviving records show beyond doubt that it was never the intention of the Germans to bomb London, but for the first time since 1918 bombs had fallen on the capital. A fire in the City of London itself was attended by 200 fire pumps and in the suburbs bombs caused extensive damage. In Bethnal Green 100 people were made homeless. Other towns and cities around the country suffered greater damage than London that night but it was the bombing of the capital that shocked Britain's leaders.

Such a mistake was understandable. Air navigation is no easy skill at the best of times; over a darkened landscape, with constant fear chafing at the brain and physical and mental exhaustion distorting the judgement, even the most reliable navigator could make a mistake. For mistake it must have been;

Bombers

By 1940 British bombers, despite Air Ministry emphasis on their strategic importance, were still primitive. Those then called 'heavy bombers' were the first twin-engined, metal-framed monoplanes to be used by the RAF. Most were larger but slower than German bombers. In daylight, they were vulnerable to Luftwaffe fighters: on 18 January, 15 Wellingtons out of 22 were lost during a daylight raid on Wilhelmshaven. But by night they were as impossible to catch as Luftwaffe bombers during the 'Blitz' and they ranged over Germany scattering bombs at will.

The Vickers Armstrong Wellington *(right)* was designed by Barnes Wallis, who later produced the dam-busting bombs. Its fabric-skinned, diagonally-framed (geodetic) construction could absorb a lot of damage but, when used later as a glider tug, could stretch as much as four inches (100mm). It was poorly armed. Its two powered turrets contained 2×.303″ Vickers machine guns with limited traverse. But its five-man crew cold deliver more than half a ton of bombs over 1000 miles (1600km). Span: 82′ 6″ (26.26m).

Length: 64′ 7″ (19.68m). 2 Bristol Pegasus 1050hp 9-cylinder radial engines gave it a top speed of 230mph (370kph).

Britain's other 'heavy' bomber was the Armstrong Whitley. First introduced in 1935, its two 795hp Armstrong Siddeley Tiger engines gave it a maximum speed of only 192mph (308kph) but it could trundle a ton of bombs more than 600 miles (950km).

'Medium' bombers included the Handley Page Hampden *(below)*, popularly known as the 'flying suitcase' because of its slim, slab-sided fuselage and narrow tail-boom. An all-metal monoplane, its twin Bristol Pegasus engines could lift 4000lb (1800kg) of bombs and gave it a top speed of 265mph (425kph) and a range of 1600 miles (2530km). It was a joy to fly; even when loaded it handled like a fighter.

no one would wittingly have disobeyed Göring's explicit orders to leave civilian targets alone. But the consequences were appalling.

The following morning Churchill toured the bomb sites and met the bombed-out families. 'Give it back to 'em,' the crowd urged him; 'See how they like it.' The Prime Minister went back to Downing Street to consider the matter. He had already discussed with senior Air Ministry officials the possibility of sending bombers to Berlin. He knew it was feasible. Already Bomber Command had flown regular raids to the industrial heartland of Germany, the Ruhr. By reducing the bombload, the aircraft's range would be extended; yes, Berlin was within reach. The Air Council agreed to send eighty bombers to

bomb Berlin that same night, the 25th, and on the 26th, and on the next few nights.

It was a significant escalation of the aerial war. In the event, after their 900-mile flight, the RAF bombers lost their way too. But enough of their bombs fell on Berlin to enrage the Führer and start Berliners clamouring for revenge. Hitler could feel justified, now, in launching deliberate raids on London. The war had taken a completely new course, suddenly veering towards new horror: the horror of Dresden, Hamburg, Cologne and finally the ultimate horror of Hiroshima and Nagasaki. All, in no small measure because someone had made a navigational error on the night of 24 August 1940.

Tactics

The day after German bombs fell on London — the first since 1918 — and the implications dawned on Berlin, Hitler righteously demanded that the aircrews responsible for the error be punished. Göring ordered them to be demoted to the infantry. In fact, however, the incident permitted German High Command to change tactics. By provoking RAF retaliation, the Luftwaffe could now claim justification for a bombing campaign against British cities. Plans were set in train for the campaign to start in early September.

Meanwhile, Berlin had been paying close attention to the progress of the air offensive. The date and final details of the invasion remained to be settled. But the invasion could not proceed until the Luftwaffe gained supremacy of British skies, and this was still very much in the balance. Cloudy weather during the four or five days up to 23 August had frustrated raids on ground targets; and, although clearer skies on the 24th allowed renewed activity against the airbases, these tactics now began to seem unnecessarily slow.

Göring and his commanders were sure, however, that the RAF was on the point of collapse. Although the Luftwaffe was consistently taking heavier losses than Fighter Command, sheer strength of numbers would keep the Germans going. What was needed was one last great effort to swamp the opposition. Mass raids would be launched not just on southern England but further north as well. Extra Bf.109s were drafted in to Kesselring's Luftflotte 2 bases to protect the huge bomber raids, while Sperrle's Luftflotte 3, deprived of fighter cover, would concentrate on night attacks.

The British, too, were reconsidering tactics. Forced, inevitably, to respond to rather than initiate action in the air, Dowding's fighter pilots were constantly lured into dogfights with the enemy's bomber escorts. The RAF's objective was primarily to stop the bombers, but with heavier and heavier escorts of Bf.109s and 110s the mass-formation raiders were too often getting through. And the pilots were exhausted. The squadrons of 11 Group, particularly, seemed to be in the air longer than there were hours in the day. Air Vice-Marshal Keith Park, head of 11 Group, was as tired as his men; and he seemed to be lacking the support of his fellow group commanders.

Keith Park was a New Zealander who had flown

with the RFC during the First World War. Formerly on Dowding's air staff, he and his chief liked and understood each other. He was able and energetic, just the man to take responsibility for the busiest group in Fighter Command. But his appointment dashed the hopes of Trafford Leigh-Mallory who instead commanded 12 Group, and there was a slight coolness between the two which tended to affect co-operation. Leigh-Mallory also criticized Park for not adopting more aggressive tactics. Fired by the suggestion of one of his squadron commanders — none other than the legless Douglas Bader, of 242 (Canadian) Squadron — Leigh-Mallory had argued that the enemy's massive formations required a more forceful response and proposed that squadrons should form up in wings of three or more, to tackle the raiders as a group.

Park's view of the idea was neutral until he sent out an urgent request for help on 24 August, and the squadrons from 12 Group arrived too late; then Park rejected the 'big wing' as simply too slow. Given enough advance warning, the wings could assemble in time to engage the enemy on equal terms, but on the south coast the raiders often struck within minutes of leaving their own bases; the defenders had no chance to do anything more elaborate than climb straight into the air. With Dowding's support, Park chose to pursue his own more measured tactics. This difference of opinion became the basis of a growing controversy that in November 1940 led to Park's removal from 11 Group; but history proved him right and he was later knighted. His priority at this crucial stage of the Battle was to protect his bases and his squadrons in southeast England.

Anatomy of a Raid

A top cover escort of Bf.109 fighters might be layered up to above 27,000ft (8300m), maybe over the bombers or on a *freijagd* (free-hunt) to clear the skies ahead.

Bombers, formed in Gruppen, could be layered up to 15,000ft (4615m) and huddled together to give protective cross-fire. As the Battle progressed, Bf.109 close escorts were tied tighter and tighter to the bombers restricting the effectiveness of the protection they were supposed to provide.

RAF fighters seldom had time to climb above the enemy fighters, and often became strung out and separated on the climb. They were thus always vulnerable to the umbrella of top-cover fighters. Later, Park tried to fly squadrons in pairs, Hurricanes to attack bombers, Spitfires taking on the Bf.109s.

To confuse the defence, the Luftwaffe often tried to slip low-level raids under British radar, planned to arrive at a target at the same time as a high-level raid for maximum surprise.

Armoury

The purpose of a fighter aircraft is to bring maximum firepower to bear on an enemy aircraft. Whatever the flying qualities of the aircraft, if it is to be used as a fighter it must be able to fight. By the Second World War such statements had become truisms: yet only twenty-five years previously the mere idea of fighter aircraft would have seemed bizarre. In early dogfights over the Western Front the combatants shot at each other with revolvers and carbines. By the end of the first war aircraft were commonly fitted with guns, but the aircraft themselves were standard machines. Design and construction improved by leaps and bounds through the thirties, until the aircraft became a dependable platform from which to attack; but, in Britain at least, armaments were neglected. In July 1934, however, a ballistics expert by the name of Captain Hill attended an Air Ministry conference to explain why he thought current armaments were obsolete. Hill reminded the Ministry that modern aircraft were so swift and agile that in combat a pilot would have just two seconds at most in which to shoot his opponents down; the logical solution was for the pilot to fire more than one gun at a time, and Hill suggested that eight would be ideal.

One of Dowding's protégés in the Ministry was Squadron Leader Ralph Sorley who strongly supported Hill's recommendations. Sorley, himself involved in research and development, favoured the American Colt Browning .303 machine gun; within a year, his enthusiasm had convinced his superiors and as a result the sophisticated new

Hurricanes and Spitfires were armed with sophisticated Brownings to match.

The two German fighters that the Hurricanes and Spitfires would meet in battle, the Bf.109s and 110s, had a mixture of machine guns and cannon. The 110s were less agile than single-seat fighters, however, and the 109s were the RAF's most usual opponents. Their two Oerlikon 20mm cannon fired explosive shells to devastating effect, but were slower and heavier and fired fewer rounds. Nevertheless, the impact of the German cannon impressed the RAF commanders, who began to look again at alternatives to the Browning.

Jointly, the eight Brownings fired a total of 160 bullets per second, each packing a 7lb (3.18kg) punch, and could continue for fifteen seconds before exhausting the ammunition. Two Oerlikon cannon fired seventeen rounds per second but were

empty within nine seconds. The Brownings were fed by flexible belts from ammunition boxes, delivering rounds of ball (solid), armour-piercing, incendiary or tracer bullets, all mixed together. Cannon shells were usually not solid; if not, the thin metal shell, drum fed to the cannon, was filled with explosive.

A few dozen Spitfires and Hurricanes underwent conversion, with two Hispano 20mm cannon fitted in place of half the Brownings; but the results were not entirely satisfactory. The guns often jammed in use, or froze at altitude. Later in the war, production models proved more satisfactory.

The armaments in turn, however, were only as efficient as the men who used them — and the men who looked after them. The armourers were highly respected members of the ground crew who worked unceasingly to clean and rearm the guns, finishing off with red patches over the gun-port holes to keep out damp; a missing patch when an aircraft returned was the tell-tale sign of action. Despite an adjustable reflector sight to help his aim, the pilot relied most on experience and correct alignment of his guns. Gun alignment was achieved by a procedure known as spot synchronization — angling the guns to converge at a certain point ahead of the aircraft. Before the war the spot was 650ft (198m) in front of the nose, but as pilots learnt to get in close for their kills they later reduced it to 200ft (61m). Split-second reactions and instinctive spatial abilities helped; but the truth was that only practice made perfect.

Sadly for novices, their only practice was an unrealistic burst or two against an air-towed windsock or a ground target. Their first real practical test was faced in the deadly skies over southern England with no diploma if they passed the test and only death if they failed.

Guns

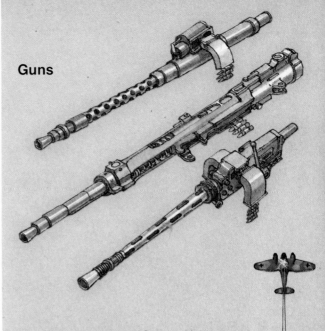

Top: Rheinmetall-Borsig MG.17 machine gun as fitted in Bf.109 and Bf.110 fighters. Length: 4′ 0″ (1.2m). Weight: 22lb (10kg). Calibre: 7.92mm. Rate of fire: 1100 rds/min. Muzzle velocity: 2450ft (783m)/sec. Belt feeding a .344oz (12.8g) bullet (1000 in fuselage; 500 in each wing).

Above centre: Oerlikon MG-FF cannon fitted in Luftwaffe fighters. Length: 4′ 1″ (1.3m). Weight: 53lb (24kg). Calibre: 20mm. Rate of fire: 520 rds/min. Muzzle velocity: 1800ft (554m)/sec. 60-round drum feeding a 4.82oz (137g) explosive shell.

Above: Browning machine gun fitted in RAF Spitfire and Hurricane fighters. Length: 3′ 8″ (1.14m). Weight: 22lb (10kg). Calibre: .303″ (7.7m) (standard army rifle size). Rate of fire: 2450 rds/min. Muzzle velocity: 2660 ft (818m)/sec. 300-round belt feeding a .34oz (9.6g) bullet.

Eight Browning .303″ (7.7mm) machine guns fired a total of 160 bullets weighing 3.5lb (1.5kg) each second. A lead weight that heavy, travelling at 1800mph (2590kph), did enormous damage to an aircraft's aluminium structure (though it was unlikely that all of a one-second burst would hit). The equal recoil through the eight fixed guns could slow a fighter considerably, and sometimes cause the aircraft to stall and spin.

Right: Spot point synchronisation of 8-gun RAF fighter set to 650 feet (198m) and 200 feet (61m) drawn to scale with a Spitfire attacking a Heinkel He.111.

Left: Deflection shooting — aiming ahead of an aircraft so that the time the bullets take to hit it matches the point the enemy flies to reach the same spot — requires instinctive judgements of speed, angle and distance. This takes long study and experience.

The Score

The score was important. It indicated the progress of the Battle. It helped to bolster confidence, or else to prompt urgent reconsideration. At the time, however, it was very difficult to check. On both sides of the Channel, pilots looked at the empty chair next to them in the mess and wondered if that man were dead, or in enemy hands, or even now nursing his damaged aircraft over the last hedge before home. Sometimes they *knew*. They saw the ball of flame engulf their chum's Spitfire, or the PAC wires that brought down the Dornier ahead. On both sides, the losses were sorely felt; the score was personal.

But the score-keepers of both sides struggled to keep an accurate tally of hits and losses, and usually got it wrong. The RAF had begun by overestimating Luftwaffe numbers, partly misled by Göring's boasts. This had the advantage of increasing Dowding's natural caution, shared by Park; both men had a tendency to prepare for the worst, not daring to hope for the best. Dowding was conscious of a developing crisis. He was losing skilled pilots at an irreplaceable rate; at the end of August 11 Group's squadrons were reduced to an average of twenty pilots, six below the full establishment. Göring, too, was issuing orders that only one experienced airman should fly in each crew; too

many were being lost. But the Luftwaffe consistently overestimated their opponents' losses, to the point where, at the end of August, they seriously thought Fighter Command was down to its last few aircraft.

In the confusion of a bombing raid, or after a wheeling dogfight; in cloud and smoke; in simple human error — it was very easy to claim a hit that never happened, or one that someone else had made. All too often a single Spitfire would be hit by the shells of three, four or five Messerschmitts, whereupon all the pilots claimed a kill. And undoubtedly, human nature being what it is, there were some who deliberately exaggerated. Indeed, the leaders themselves exaggerated for propaganda purposes and to bolster morale. No one believed the other side's claims, but most people did believe their own side. The national newspapers gloated cheerfully that so many enemy aircraft had been lost the day before 'for the loss of only...' and readers registered this information as a fact just like the time the black-out would begin.

Despite the confusion, however, certain patterns were discernible by now. Fine weather brought heavy bombing raids; the more aircraft were involved, the more aircraft were lost. The Luftwaffe lost more bombers than fighters. Bombers, having larger crews, suffered longer casualty lists. As most of the encounters took place over Britain, RAF survivors who parachuted out of a damaged aircraft

LOSSES	1940			
	10–31 July	1–31 August	1–30 September	To the end of the year
Fighter Command aircrew killed	68	176	173	120
Fighter aircraft lost	91	389	358	185
Luftwaffe aircrew lost	348	993	829	492
Luftwaffe aircraft lost	185	694	629	379

TOTAL LOSSES	
Fighter Command airmen killed	537
Bf.109 and Bf.110 crew lost	551
Other Luftwaffe crew lost	2,111
Royal Air Force fighter aircraft lost	1,023
Bf.109s and Bf.110s lost	873
Luftwaffe bombers lost	1,014

could be back with their squadrons that same day; German survivors invariably ended as prisoners of war. One or two German aircrew managed to evade capture for a few days — the record was nine days in deepest Berkshire — but most were swept into POW camps after interrogation.

The RAF airmen who parachuted back to earth faced less humiliation but more exhaustion. Drawn back to their base squadron by the knowledge of desperate pilot shortages and by the sheer warmth of camaraderie, some of them survived a whole lifetime's experiences within a few hours. Scrambling to meet the raiders, narrowly missing one, hearing the engine falter and seeing the flames lick up around your feet ... smashing at the jammed cockpit cover — again, again — then tumbling out and falling, losing the D-ring on the parachute, finding it, drifting quietly ... watching the black smoke rise from the wreckage of your Hurricane. Landing in a Kent field, gathering up your parachute and hitching a ride with the vicar into town, conscious that your clothes reek of high-octane fuel. Arriving back at base with an odd sense of anticlimax, knowing you will soon be climbing into another Hurricane, and may soon repeat this day's adventures ...

The courage and gritty determination displayed by such RAF pilots was equalled only by their German counterparts, who faced the extra hazard of the Channel.

Recovery

The Luftwaffe, designed to fight in the skies over the European land mass, was remarkably well equipped to fight over water. Each pilot had, in addition to his parachute, an inflatable life-jacket, a rubber dinghy and a bag of dye to stain the water bright green. Furthermore, a systematic air–sea rescue service had been started, the *Seenotflugkommando*, which included fleets of Heinkel 59 seaplanes and high-speed motor launches, and Ernst Udet, one of Göring's senior aides, had taken a personal interest in developing a kind of buoy-cum-lifeboat in which survivors could shelter until help arrived. For the waters of the Channel and the North Sea, even in high summer, could be lethally cold.

In October strange buoys were spotted in mid-Channel with large Red Cross markings painted on a top shaped like a conning tower. On investigation these were found to be German rescue floats and they were equipped with everything a downed airman might require. There were first aid kits, blankets, food, water and distress signals sufficient for four men. There were even games to entertain the occupants and bungs to plug any leaks. These 'lobster pots', as they became known, provided a life-saving refuge for more than one RAF pilot. Capture and imprisonment for the duration was, however, inevitable if one of the German patrol craft should call to check for visitors, as they did regularly.

The RAF, by comparison, had only the barest essentials: the 'Mae West' life-jacket and a trusting faith in the Royal National Lifeboat Institution. Dowding had recognized the need for a special rescue service; he continually badgered the Air Ministry for money and men to set one up, but managed to get only sixteen fast launches before the Battle began, based in the southeast. More often it was fishermen that went to the rescue; they braved minefields and strafing to reach friend and foe alike, sometimes squabbling for the honour of saving a Fighter Command pilot or the glory of sailing back into harbour with a live German.

Admittedly RAF aircrew had the advantage of the quick-release parachute harness: a single tap on the buckle and the harness was free. Designed so that men were not dragged along the ground by a billowing parachute after landing, the quick-release harness was even more welcome when aircrew dropped into the sea; the silken folds and lines could easily pull a man under. It was also a source of comfort to men who feared a long, slow, agonized descent — a potential quick-release from life itself.

The decision to abandon an aircraft was never taken lightly. Aircrew on both sides were warned of the difficulty of rescue, particularly at sea, and the point never had to be laboured. If any hope remained, most pilots preferred to hold out for a possible emergency landing, nursing their shattered aircraft down over cliff-tops and beaches. But ditching a fighter was inherently risky: the slim, nose-heavy fuselage with gaping radiator intakes underneath tended to sink with astonishing speed. One man who survived after ditching, Norman Ryder, later reported how the water swilled green

into the cockpit, then darkened ominously; when it turned black, he told his friends, he knew it was time to jettison the canopy and get out. He was famous thereafter as 'Green to Black' Ryder.

More often, however, the decision was unavoidable and a pilot had just seconds to bale out, whether over land or sea was unimportant. Facing a dunking, aircrew dangling from their parachutes and drifting silently down to the sea tried to recall what the instructors had told them. Take your bearings and note any landmarks. Be alert for fishing boats. Remove excess clothing: helmet, oxygen mask, boots. Pray. Once in the water, even a mild swell hid everything from sight, and one bobbing head was hard to find. Maybe you were lucky; maybe you were uninjured and near enough to the coast to swim ashore, or found strong hands pulling you onto the deck of a trawler whose crew saw your fall. Then you would return to base with a good tale for your chums: 'Piece of cake,' you might tell them, still euphoric at your good fortune, though the nightmares would bring it back later.

Too many men were not lucky. Bodies were washed up on a lonely beach or pebble shore, days or weeks after being officially posted 'Missing'. And many others escaped death only to suffer mutilation and appalling injuries.

The 'Mae West' Life Jacket

The 'Mae West' life jacket was so constructed that it had enough buoyancy to turn an unconscious airman on his back and support him with his face held above the water.

The ASR Launch

Only a handful of these powerful motorboats, known by the RAF as High Speed Launches, were available in 1940. They were equipped with machine guns for defence against air attack. They were seventy feet in length and could make up to 30 knots.

In the Drink

The RAF had paid scanty attention to rescue services as it was not foreseen that combat would take place over the English Channel France was the place where any battle would be fought. During July, over 200 airmen perished at sea. Those that were lucky were picked up by the Royal Navy, merchant vessels or fishing boats. Air searches were made by Coastal Command Ansons and Army Co-operation and Command Lysanders, but these had no direct way of effecting a rescue and could only alert shipping in the area.

The Luftwaffe, on the other hand, had a specialist air–sea rescue organization known as the *Seenotdienst*. This was equipped with 169 sea planes which carried rubber boats, medical supplies and radio sets. These aircraft could land on the sea to effect a rescue or summon fast launches. By the end of the Battle, rafts had been moored in mid-Channel and were fully equipped with supplies and survival equipment.

Luftwaffe aircrew carried maximum protection on each flight. Even lone fighter pilots shot down over the sea could, if uninjured, rely on their parachutes for a safe descent into the sea. They could then depend on an automatically inflated yellow rubber dinghy and, once safely aboard, could use a packet of dye which stained the water a bright green to attract the attention of rescuers. Although at first derided as unnecessary by many Fighter Command pilots, a similar dinghy was quickly developed by the RAF, and helped to save many aircrew lives.

Injury to Insult

Some men baled out of their stricken aircraft and landed without a scratch. Others died instantly. But many more suffered terrible injuries, escaping death by the narrowest of margins and then facing years, perhaps a lifetime, of pain, disability and disfigurement.

The pilots of Fighter Command, like their German counterparts, were young men in their early twenties; some, indeed, were still in their teens. And for the most part they shared that healthy, youthful attitude of 'It couldn't happen to me.' Yet at some level everyone knew that it *could* happen to him, that death might strike at any moment — but that controlling fear was part of the job. You were helped by the camaraderie, the warmth of friendship in the mess: a slap on the back could jolt you out of momentary panic, a game of cards could help you forget your qualms. You each had your own way of coping with internal fears. Some of your companions could banish the doubt through sheer force of will, seeming to have not a care in the world. Some were helped by religious beliefs; some by observing superstitious rituals. But most of you managed just by keeping busy: joining the boys in the mess for a drink, chatting up the WAAF telephonist, indulging in banter or just intense games of chess.

Despite their apparent fragility, the aircraft were surprisingly sturdy. Many a pilot managed an emergency landing with his 'crate' as full of

holes as a colander, for the stressed metal airframes stood up to considerable punishment. But if one of the more sensitive areas was hit — the engine, fuel tanks, control surfaces — then the real trouble began. Fire was the greatest threat. In both Spitfires and Hurricanes a fuel tank lay between engine and cockpit, with only a thin bulkhead protecting the pilot; and the Bf.109 had its tank shaped to fit under and behind the pilot's seat. British or German, the pilot might suddenly find himself engulfed in a fiery explosion, seared by temperatures that could melt clothes, flesh, everything in seconds.

Sergeant F. S. Perkin was shot down over London on 23 September. He baled out of his Hurricane and landed in the sea near the Thames Estuary. 'Suddenly there was an explosion and my whole cockpit was enveloped in flames. A petrol flame is more intense, hotter and fiercer than almost any other fire I know of. In the Hurricane, you had the reserve tank of petrol right in front of you, in between the engine and the cockpit. You had that straight in your face.'

You can only think, "I must get out of this." People who stayed in a burning cockpit for ten seconds were overcome by the flames and the heat. Nine seconds and you ended up in … a burns surgery [unit] for the rest of the war. If you got out in eight seconds, you never flew again, but went back about twelve times for plastic surgery.' Perkin got out in four or five seconds but found himself hanging by his oxygen and radio leads, both of which were attached to his helmet. Eventually his helmet was torn off and he escaped without serious injury.

In theory it was easy enough to escape, so long as the aircraft was stable. You unhooked the RT and oxygen leads (otherwise they might strangle you), slid back the canopy, unfastened your straps, pushed the stick forward and with luck got plucked out by the air currents. When clear of the aircraft, you pulled the rip cord and heard the snap of silk filling out; then silence as you drifted slowly down to earth. Yet even now there was a risk of being shot down by the opposition's machine guns, while hanging in mid-air. Dowding had firm views on this; whereas German aircrew should be considered POWs from the moment they baled out, RAF pilots were fair game, as they could be back in battle and killing German pilots within hours.

In practice, however, escape from a damaged aircraft was never easy, especially when a man was already wounded. Increasingly, hospitals all over southern Britain were seeing new kinds of injuries. Shrapnel and bullet wounds were to be expected; but never before had there been so many broken necks and spines, caused by damaged parachutes and crash landings, and particularly the terrible burns. Survivors told of seeing their own flesh bubble and blister while they fought to escape the flames; often, the pain did not arrive till later. On the ground, rescuers did their even-handed best for friend and foe; German aircrew later reported their surprise at the kindness they received. But very few doctors understood how to treat burn patients; all they could do was offer painkillers while nature helped the body to heal itself. There was one man, however, at a Sussex hospital, who had just begun to specialize in treating burns: Archibald McIndoe.

McIndoe accepted as many as possible of the patients considered untreatable elsewhere. His techniques were still experimental, he warned every new patient; they might not work and they would certainly increase the short-term suffering. He called his patients 'guinea pigs'. But, encouraged by their fellow sufferers, they underwent McIndoe's ministrations with the same fortitude and bantering humour that had helped them face the apprehension at the airfield, and in the end they were rewarded with new faces, fingers that worked, and other miracles of plastic surgery. By then, however, many more burns victims would have reached the unit, for at the end of August 1940 the Battle of Britain entered a new stage of intensity.

Caterpillars and Guinea Pigs

Leslie L. Irvin was an American high-diver who became interested in parachutes before the First World War. He recognized the potential dangers of the static-line parachute then in standard use and developed his own design, to be opened manually by the parachutist. At first his efforts were mocked; contemporary wisdom said that a falling body would lose consciousness. But he reasoned that if a high-diver could control his will during a 100ft (30m) dive, a parachutist could tug a cord while falling. And in 1919 he proved his theory, and his design, by jumping from an aircraft. He set up a company to supply civil and service aviators worldwide, including the USAAF and the RAF. By the Second World War his parachutes had been used for over 100,000 jumps, and thousands of lives had been saved — the latter then becoming eligible for membership of the Caterpillar Club, whose badge depicted a silkworm.

The Irvin parachute was a circular silk canopy 24ft (7.32m) in diameter, with sixteen rigging lines. The lines were divided and spliced to four D-rings, clipped into the harness buckle ('release box') with a boss which, when given a quarter turn and knocked, would instantly release the rigging lines. A sharp pull on the rip cord broke ties holding the pack together, allowing a small pilot chute to pull out and deploy the canopy.

Archibald McIndoe was born in 1900 in Dunedin, New Zealand. Qualifying as a doctor in New Zealand, he moved to London in 1930 to work under Sir Harold Gillies, a plastic surgeon. He set up his special burns unit at the Queen Victoria Hospital, East Grinstead, in 1939. At the time, treatment of burns usually involved tannic acid or animal fat: not much use where soft tissue, muscle, cartilage or sinew has been destroyed. McIndoe pioneered not merely the replacement of skin but the rebuilding of whole faces or limbs by grafting tissue from unburnt areas. His patients — they formed themselves into the Guinea Pig Club — regarded him with respect and affection, and applauded his knighthood in 1947.

Against the Ropes

The number and the ferocity of dogfights over Britain were increasing, and on both sides the losses soared. In the first week of August, the Luftwaffe lost 26 aircraft, the RAF 3; in the second week the figures had leapt to 169 and 99 respectively; in the third week, 221 and 88. But, by late August, the Luftflotte commanders had learnt that their best chance lay in swamping the RAF, by attacking not piecemeal but en masse and by concentrating on fewer targets. Now the pilots of Fighter Command would take even greater punishment as the Battle entered a new stage of intensity.

Dowding was already anxious. At this rate Fighter Command could not hold out much longer; he simply did not have the pilots or the aircraft to replace those being lost. In the ten days to 18 August, 95 pilots had been killed and another 60 injured; and over the next ten days those figures would more than double. The bases were being severely battered, the all-important sector stations — Debden, Hornchurch, Biggin Hill, for instance — but also forward bases like Manston. The ops rooms were particularly vulnerable, built as they often were above ground; even protected by blast walls, their operations were often interrupted. Airfields were peppered with craters and unexploded bombs; more and more often, stations would have to close and squadrons divert for a few hours, while ground staff repaired damage. Power and communications lines were frequently disrupted. And all over the country, from Plymouth in the west to Norwich in the east, and north as far as Merseyside, Yorkshire, even Scotland, the enemy bombers were getting through, plastering cities with incendiaries and high explosive and leaving death in their wake.

Now the enemy sorties were even more massive: up to 1000 aircraft flying across the Channel daily, only to divide into four or five formations over Britain, confusing the radar operators and squadron controllers. And by night the mass bombing continued: industrial targets in the Midlands, docks at Liverpool and Southampton, naval bases, railway centres, and of course the airfields. There had been sporadic nightly raids before, but nothing on

this scale. Attacking in such numbers, inevitably some of the bombers managed to get through. British scientists were still developing Airborne Interception, the airborne version of radar which would help fighters to locate the enemy at night; but until AI was in use (late in 1940), the RAF's fighters were effectively blindfold in the dark.

Although the occasional bomber was brought down at night this was usually the result of very bad luck on the part of the German crew. Several bombers had collided with balloon cables and one or two of them had crashed. A few had been hit by anti-aircraft fire, but there was just as much chance of running out of fuel or getting lost. A handful had been shot down by night fighters, but the first successful use of AI did not happen until the night of 19 November 1940, when Flight Lieutenant Cunningham, later to be christened 'Cat's Eyes', shot down a Ju.88 attacking Birmingham.

The pressure on Dowding's pilots was intense and unrelenting, continuing from day into night. But it was not just the pilots who were working overtime. Ground crews had refined their service technique to match the urgency of the time: waiting in slit trenches beside the landing grounds they swarmed over incoming aircraft before the exhausted pilots could clamber out, to change oxygen cylinders and run oil, coolant and RT checks, to refuel, replace ammunition and effect minor repairs, sometimes by torchlight. Thanks to their efforts, a whole squadron could be turned round in as little as ten minutes. The Army provided bomb disposal experts to defuse unexploded bombs and manual labour to straighten damaged buildings and craters. Civilians, too, played their part: engineers, for example, who doggedly repaired telephone, gas, water or electrical links, despite the constant risk of air raids.

At the end of August, as the fickle weather turned to blue skies, the enemy was clearly intent upon extinguishing the RAF. Keith Park regretfully acknowledged the possibility that his 11 Group might have to withdraw to bases further north. While Britain stepped up preparations for the invasion that would surely follow, he preserved his pilots for the last great offensive, refusing to let them respond to provocation from Göring's fighters. As far as possible, he held his fire. What mattered was that his pilots should recover their strength in time for the final, critical stage of the Battle.

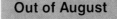

Out of August

In the middle of August, Hitler and Göring changed the course of the battle by striking directly at RAF bases. The intention was to win air superiority over southeast Britain by destroying the RAF's aircraft on the ground or in the air, and to reduce Fighter Command's bases and communications to a level where they could not oppose the planned Sealion invasion.

13 August, Adlertag. The Luftwaffe's plan to 'destroy the RAF in four days' became a shambles when bad weather caused a last-minute cancellation of the morning raid. Aircraft already airborne failed to hear the recall; bombers attacked without escorts, while some escorts lost their bombers. Afternoon raids were more successful.

14 August. Luftwaffe continued attacks on southeast airfields and railways. Middle Wallop hit. RAF losses: 8. Luftwaffe losses: 19.

15 August. Good weather promoted an all-out effort. The Luftwaffe flew 1786 sorties, of which 520 were by bombers. They provoked 874 RAF sorties. For the first and last time, Luftflotte 5 in Scandinavia took part and were surprised to find that not all Dowding's fighters had been sent south; they were met and trounced by 12 and 13 Group aircraft. RAF losses: 35. Luftwaffe losses: 75.

16 August. The attacks on airfields begun the previous day continued with Manston, West Malling, Harwell and Farnborough being bombed. At Tangmere, Stukas put the important airfield out of action. Fleet Air Arm aircraft were destroyed at Lee-on-Solent, and at Brize Norton 46 training aircraft were wrecked. The RDF (Radar) station at Ventnor on the Isle of Wight was put out of action and bombs fell in southeast London.

17 August. Despite ideal weather conditions only a few reconnaissance aircraft were sent out.

18 August. After a day's rest the Luftwaffe returned in force to bomb the airfields once more. Do.17s of KG76 put on a textbook low-level raid which put Kenley out of action. Croydon, Biggin Hill, West Malling, Gosport, Thorney Island, Ford and Manston were also bombed.

19 August. The Luftwaffe occupied itself with reconnaissance sorties to assess the effects of their efforts.

24 August. The attacks on airfields were renewed. Manston put out of action. North Weald and Hornchurch bombed. At night London was bombed.

25 August. The Luftwaffe waited until late afternoon before making their attacks. At night a large number of bombs fell in the Midlands.

26 August. Kenley, Biggin Hill, Hornchurch, North Weald, Debden and Warmwell airfields attacked. At night Coventry and Birmingham were bombed.

30 August. Shipping in the Thames Estuary attacked by over 100 aircraft. Detling, Kenley, Biggin Hill and North Weald heavily attacked — a tremendous battle was fought over Surrey.

31 August. One of the hardest-fought days of the Battle started with Bf.109s shooting down all the barrage balloons at Dover. Debden and North Weald were bombed. 100 aircraft bombed Eastchurch. Croydon was attacked, Hornchurch and Biggin Hill put out of action. Radar stations around the coast attacked. Fighter Command lost 41 aircraft, but only 9 pilots; the Luftwaffe lost 39 aircraft and 21 aircrew.

Resting

The Battle was at its height, but Dowding had no idea how long this crisis would last. Acting on instincts derived from his experience in the First World War, he had urged his group commanders — above all, Park — to rotate their squadrons from front-line activity to the comparative calm of rearguard bases. And Park heeded his advice.

The pilots of the 11 Group squadrons were exhausted. The physical strain was bad enough. Nearly every day brought a renewed frenzy of death-defying clashes in the sky, often more than once a day. Fortunately, the body seemed to take over at times, to continue automatically; sometimes an aircraft taxied to a halt and ground crew found the pilot slumped over the controls, asleep. But the mental strain was the killer: the strain of seeing your friends and comrades die like flies around you, swatted out of the sky; the strain of knowing that you could be next.

The Luftwaffe pilots were exhausted too. This new stage of the Battle, with no holds barred, was taking a toll on everyone. Despite their own side's propaganda, the German aircrew knew that Fighter Command was not yet finished; the RAF pilots still fought with grim resolve. Moreover, the pilots of the Bf.109s were indignant at being confined to close escort duties for the bombing raids; they wanted the

autonomy to roam singly or in small packs, luring the Hurricanes and Spitfires into skirmishes and attacking the RAF's bases at will. But as yet their arguments had failed to convince Göring.

On both sides, fatigue manifested itself in mistakes, sometimes with fatal consequences. Errors of navigation caused bombs to be dropped short of their target. Misreading of instruments caused sudden fuel shortages, enforcing a return to base. Tired eyes missed the tell-tale glint of sun on a perspex canopy, swooping out of the cloud above. On both sides, mistakes caused losses that were increasingly unacceptable. But Luftwaffe organization did not allow for rotation of *Staffeln*, even when front-line units were in desperate need of rest. Official leave followed a strict and inflexible rota; normally they were expected to fly every mission that was called.

This approach of leaving operational fighter pilots in the front line rather than rotating them led to some men running up huge numbers of victories. These 'Experten', as they were called in Germany, were treated as heroes and their photographs were published in magazines such as *Der Adler*, the Luftwaffe's house publication. The most successful German fighter pilot at this time was Major Werner Molders of JG51, one of only three pilots to be awarded the Ritterkreuz during the Battle of Britain, the others being Adolf Galland and Helmut Wick. Even though based in France, a country which only weeks before had been the enemy, the Luftwaffe aircrew cut dashing figures and were quickly accepted by many natives as part of the scene. They ate and drank in the cafés, danced and dated the local girls. They also enjoyed the luxury of opulent billets — in requisitioned châteaux or comfortable Normandy farmhouses.

Just two or three score miles away, beneath the same hot summer sun, the pilots of Fighter Command were often billeted in corrugated steel Nissen huts or ramshackle barns, accommodation on their airbase having long since been destroyed. Even when withdrawn according to Dowding's scheme, they were hardly rewarded with luxury. Indeed, the 'rest' they now enjoyed was no frivolous dallying in whatever backwater to which they had been sent; they still faced hours of patrolling over North Sea convoys, and regular confrontations with enemy reconnaissance aircraft. Besides, apart from days when the weather closed in completely, when they could truly relax with pets and card games and trips to the local pubs, the experienced pilots were required to share their hard-won knowledge with the new boys.

The new pilots were being swept through training school with almost indecent haste. Even the volunteers from Coastal Command, the Fleet Air Arm and other flying units needed instruction in aerial combat, having undergone a mere six-day conversion course to accustom them to the idiosyncrasies of Spitfires and Hurricanes and to teach them the basics of gunnery. On joining the operational squadron to which they had been assigned, they required many patient sessions in the air, learning confidence in their machines and themselves, developing 'fighter pilot's eye', imbibing the wisdom of those who had fought in earnest — above all, learning discipline, the self-control required

of those who work in a team. One vital lesson was caution and precision in the use of radio: the cry 'Look out behind you!', no matter how well meaning, guaranteed that all pilots in hearing distance would fling their machines across the sky, when a more appropriate warning might be 'Red Three calling Red Leader: four 109s at three o'clock below', or 'Break, Red Three', or even 'Look out behind you, Pete!'.

All too soon the eager new faces would have joined the re-formed squadron for its return to the forefront of the Battle. Ill-trained, short of experience and confidence, but endowed with youthful high spirits and enormous courage, they would soon be meeting increasingly unfavourable odds.

Out of August

The first week of September brought a continuation of the blue skies of August — and a continuation of the assault on British airfields by day and industry by night. Göring was jubilant. Now the Luftwaffe had a chance to fulfil his boasts, to exterminate the RAF. On 29 August, in fact, one of Kesselring's subordinates, General von Döring, had announced that the Luftwaffe had already won air supremacy over Britain. All the British forward bases had suffered extensive damage. RAF losses of aircraft and pilots could not be sustained much longer. Industrial centres, especially the all-important aircraft production lines, were badly disrupted by German bombs. Göring assumed that the great air assault, the preliminary to invasion, was nearly complete.

But Göring's optimism was misplaced. Luftwaffe estimates of the British position were broadly correct — but, as usual, overstated. His own pilots could tell him the truth: after six weeks of the Battle of Britain, there was still

considerable fight left in Fighter Command. On 2 September, Göring asked Adolf Galland, one of his finest young fighter commanders, what more he needed to complete the job, and Galland is alleged to have replied: 'A squadron of Spitfires.' Furious, the Reichsmarschall rounded on his fighter pilots, berating them for letting down the bombers. Galland had in fact been referring to the Spitfire's supposed superiority as an escort aircraft; he and his comrades were generally very satisfied with their Bf.109s, but could never forget that the Bf.109 had been designed for *freijagd* operations, for fighting with a free hand, not for close escort duties.

Dowding and Park, on the other hand, were under no illusions. On the last day of August the

RAF had lost thirty-nine aircraft, the highest daily total so far (and, as it transpired, the highest of the Battle). Some squadrons were flying up to five sorties a day. The 11 Group sector stations were still open, but only just; some of the ops rooms had to be moved, in some cases off the station itself — Biggin Hill's ops room now occupied a nearby butcher's shop. From interrogation of German prisoners of war, it seemed that the Luftwaffe could continue to absorb its current high level of losses, and still take the offensive over Britain.

Sunday, 1 September brought a resumption of the mass raids on Biggin Hill, Kenley, Hornchurch and other sector stations. The radar installation at Dunkirk, near Canterbury, was also attacked. The depleted 11 Group squadrons battled valiantly with the invaders, but with meagre results. Monday the 2nd saw even heavier raids: altogether the enemy launched nearly a thousand sorties, mainly targeted on southeast England.

The first raid came at 0700 hours. Amongst the airfields attacked were Rochford, Eastchurch and North Weald, while a low-level raid was made on Biggin Hill by nine Dorniers. Three more raids were launched later in the day, one at noon and two in the afternoon, and in each case the main targets were airfields. The rest of the week continued in like vein. This was clearly the Luftwaffe's preparation for an invasion. Dowding and his group commanders began to plan for 11 Group's withdrawal to more northerly bases, and for a wholescale reorganization of Fighter Command, reassigning squadrons according to three categories: first, those who could continue the front-line battles; second, reserves to bolster the first group; and third, rearguard squadrons where a core of experienced men could augment the training of new pilots, until they were fit to join one of the other two groups.

The likely effect on morale would not be positive. Squadron loyalties had been a major source of strength, permitting the growth of friendships and trust, the framework for team success. Now the bonds between individual pilots, and between ground crews and pilots, would be lost. Acknowledging all this, Dowding and his senior commanders nevertheless continued to develop the plan. They weren't to know that on 7 September, the very day they announced the reorganization, Hitler and Göring would solve half their problems for them by switching the Luftwaffe's raids from the airfields to the cities.

Bloody Harvest

1–6 September. Although the pattern of attacks during the first week of September appeared the same to Fighter Command as they desperately defended their bases, changes were already in the wind. Göring and his staff were planning their attacks on London just as Dowding and Park, contemplating their tattered forces, were seriously considering a retreat from 11 Group to 12 Group stations north of London. This would have left the invasion beaches unprotected. 466 RAF fighters had been lost or damaged between 24 August and 6 September. Worse still, 230 pilots had been killed or injured. The remainder were utterly weary and battle-fatigued. Despite the effect on morale, it was decided to reform squadrons into three categories: A) front-line operational with the best and most experienced pilots, B) second-class operational reserves, and C) reforming or training under experienced leaders. While this was going on, those in the front line continued to fight off raids, which daily damaged airfields and aircraft factories. RAF losses: 110. Luftwaffe losses: 148.

7 September. Morning raids on airfields. In the afternoon Park visited Bentley Priory. In his absence, an afternoon raid which ignored airfields and headed directly for London caught controllers unprepared, with fighters patrolling in the wrong places. Göring had taken personal command of the raids on London, and was on Cap Gris Nez to watch 300 plus bombers and 600 plus fighters cross the coast. Bombs carpeted the docks, the East End and south London. Fires were still burning at night as huge beacons to guide a later night raid. 306 Londoners died. Invasion alert sounded, church bells rung and Home Guard mustered. RAF losses: 25. Luftwaffe losses: 41.

8 September. Both sides rested, licking their wounds, and there was little activity.

9 September. The Luftwaffe attempted to repeat the London raid, but was foiled by Fighter Command. A night raid killed a further 412 Londoners. RAF losses: 17. Luftwaffe losses: 30.

10–14 September. Bad weather brought daytime respite, but London was bombed by night.

15 September. Battle of Britain Day. Two massive raids, one in the morning and another in the afternoon, drive for London. Both successfully intercepted by 23 RAF squadrons, but fires lit the way for a night raid. RAF losses: 26. Luftwaffe losses: 60 (but the RAF claimed 183 initially).

27 September. Activity began with raids on London by Bf.109s and Bf.110s, but these were fought off with heavy losses incurred by the raiders. In the afternoon a force of 80 bombers and fighters made for Bristol and were again beaten off. At the same time 300 aircraft made for London and were engaged south of the city by large numbers of fighters which turned them back. Losses: RAF — 28 aircraft and 20 pilots; Luftwaffe — 57 aircraft and 81 aircrew.

Office Hours

You are woken by a batman bringing a hot sweet cup of tea. For a moment you wonder where you are. Then the twinge in your neck reminds you; the tension is still in your muscles. You are just nineteen, barely a year out of school, but already a veteran of three weeks. You had been based in Lincolnshire, now you've been moved down to 'some place in Kent' as you told your parents in a letter yesterday. What you didn't tell them, but what they can probably guess for themselves, is that this is the front line in the Battle for Britain. And the airfield certainly bears the scars; some chaps are even living in tents, until the accommodation block can be rebuilt.

As you run a razor — scarcely necessary — over your chin, a sunbeam dances in the mirror and reminds you this fine September day will bring the enemy bombers for sure. A momentary thrill runs down your spine, then grips your stomach. Willing the nervous thoughts away, you remind yourself that you owe Lofty ten bob; that was a good session in the bar last night. In the mess for breakfast of leathery eggs and bacon, you overhear a muttered conversation between two of the older men; you catch the words '...bought it over the Channel'. Swallowing hard, you nearly choke on a slice of bread and marmalade; but you are young and healthy and you need your food. The Tannoy crackles into life.

'Dingo Squadron at readiness... Dingo Squadron at readiness.'

You join the general move towards the dispersal hut, where you'll get the latest gen. Flight announces that you're flying Blue Two in B flight, and your Spitfire is 'G'; he gives you Form 700 to sign, saying you can't see any holes. Now you wait. It is 0800 hours and there is a faint haze over the airfield; it's going to be another scorcher today. Some of the chaps take their deckchairs outside, joshing each other to hide their nerves. You and Lofty get out the chess board; you're just setting up the pieces when the telephone rings. An expectant silence, then the clerk yells: 'Dingo Squadron, scramble! Dingo Squadron...' You're on your way. Grab helmet, run. Grass is slippery with dew. Mind you don't slip on the wing. Leg over the side, into the cockpit, straps on, RT and oxygen leads plugged in. A quick check and raise your thumb to Whatsisname down on the ground. Switch on. The prop jerks round: one, two, three blades, now merged into a shining disc.

For a second you sit there, registering the sound, vibration, the fumes and rising heat from the engine. then you're bouncing over the rough grass after Blue One, pulling the canopy shut. The controller's voice comes over the RT: 'Kirby... Woodruff calling Kirby. I have some trade for you — sixty-plus over Maidstone. Climb vector 140 to angels 25. Buster!' You swing into the wind, keeping an eye on Blue One on your right and Red Section already climbing ahead, then ease back on the stick. A last isolated bounce and the ground falls away. Change hands to get the undercarriage up.

Check instruments and sight, switch guns on, adjust seat height, all the time swivelling your eyes around the sky.

For what seems like an age you climb. Past the odd, whispy cloud and up into the blinding sun at 25,000 feet.

'Red Three to Kirby. Bandits above at four o'clock.'

'I see them, Red Three.'

You see them too: hundreds of black dots, glinting in the sun. Another layer above them. Vapour trails betraying a third layer even higher up.

'Kirby to Woodruff. Tally ho! Blue and Green sections, get the bombers. Red and Yellow sections, follow me. We'll keep those fighters off.'

The knot in your stomach is forgotten in the sudden burst of activity. Your earphones are filled with a cacophony of voices. 'Watch out, Red Leader: above.' 'I see them. Watch out behind, Red Four.' 'Christ, that was close.' 'Red Three, break port, break port.' 'Whew, this is getting dangerous.' 'I think I got him...'

'Look out, Blue Two — behind you.' *Blue Two.* Ye gods, that's you! You slam the stick and rudder over. Two loud bangs. The Spitfire bucks, the stick jerks out of your hand. The cockpit fills with acrid smoke. A shadow flashes overhead, so close you duck. You sense, rather than see, that it's a Bf.109.

'Blue Two here. I've been hit. Can you get the bastard?'

'All clear, Blue Two. Can you make it back?'

'I think so.' At least the RT's okay. The engine's been hit, though. Switch off, canopy back to clear the smoke. Ah, there's the base. You can make it from here, just flatten your glide path a bit. Undercarriage down. 'Blue Two to Kirby Base...' There: all's well that ends well. A tug is waiting to pull you back to the repair shop.

'Sorry, Flight, bit of a mess,' you comment as he stands beside you, inspecting the holes in the rear fuselage and tail. 'Certainly is,' he agrees. 'Why didn't you bale out, then we could have got a new one! Never mind, we'll get you ... let's see, Number 237 should be ready. Yes, that'll do. Shouldn't wonder if you're not off again soon.'

The last of the dew is still glittering on the grass. Somewhere a blackbird is singing throatily. Where is that German pilot now? Did the bombers get through? Will you get another crack at them, and if so will you get back safely again? It's 1015 hours: time for a cuppa in the mess. Let's see if that WAAF telegraphist is around...

Change of Direction

It was mid-afternoon on Saturday, 7 September, another fine, clear, warm day. Göring, accompanied by Kesselring and some of his staff officers, was standing on the French cliffs opposite Dover. He had arrived in the Pas de Calais in his private train, and driven the last few miles in an open Mercedes. He wanted to witness the start of the 'reprisal raids' that the Führer had ordered, back on 30 August. Still smarting from the humiliation of RAF bombers reaching Berlin, albeit with only pinprick effect, Hitler had finally decided to launch an all-out attack on London. The offensive would simultaneously deliver the coup de grâce to the crumbling remnants of Fighter Command and strike terror into the heart of the British nation. The invasion itself was now scheduled for 21 September, exactly a fortnight away.

Eagerly the Reichsmarschall awaited the 'historic hour', as he described it to an attendant radio reporter, giving undue emphasis to his own role in the operation: 'I now want to take this opportunity of speaking to you, to say that this moment is an historic one. As a result of the provocative British attacks on Berlin on recent nights, the Führer has ordered a mighty blow to be struck in revenge against the capital of the British Empire. I personally have assumed the leadership of this attack. For the first time the victorious Luftwaffe is even now driving towards the heart of the enemy in broad daylight. The enemy defences have been beaten down and the target reached. I am certain that our success has been as great as the boldness of the plan and the fighting spirit of our crews deserves. In any event this is an historic hour, in which for the first time the Luftwaffe has struck at the heart of the enemy.'

The minutes ticked past. Göring's impatience grew. He fiddled with his binoculars. Then there came the unmistakable growl of distant aircraft, hundreds of them, approaching the coast from inland. At last they appeared, the bombers circling slowly overhead while the fighter escorts took up their positions, filling the air with deafening noise and the men below with awe. It was a huge aerial armada. Altogether there were 650 bombers and 350 fighters: an unswerving mass, heading for London.

By 1600 hours the foremost raiders were sweeping over the Kent coast. Park was at Bentley Priory; he had urgent matters to discuss with Dowding. It had been a quiet morning, surprisingly; with these clear skies the Spitfires and Hurricanes were ready and waiting for action. Park left his Uxbridge controllers in charge. At Stanmore he found Fighter Command HQ on a special alert: the King and Queen were visiting Bentley Priory that very afternoon. As the news broke, Dowding was torn between his desire to welcome the royal visitors and his urge to watch events unfolding in his operations room; 'I must have seemed a distracted host,' he said later.

Radar operators had, of course, reported the huge formation massing over the French coast, but on reaching Kent the single formation split, as if the Luftwaffe intended making several simultaneous raids on bases to north and south of the Thames. The 11 Group controllers had already scrambled their fighters: at Kenley, Northolt, Hendon, North Weald, Hornchurch, Biggin Hill and elsewhere, Hurricanes and Spitfires were already circling in readiness. But they had assumed the enemy was returning to attack the airfields.

Gradually it dawned on the defenders both in the air and on the ground that the Luftwaffe had changed its objective. This time the target was London. It was too late to save the East End

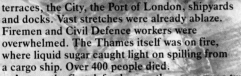

terraces, the City, the Port of London, shipyards and docks. Vast stretches were already ablaze. Firemen and Civil Defence workers were overwhelmed. The Thames itself was on fire, where liquid sugar caught light on spilling from a cargo ship. Over 400 people died.

Among the first defenders on the scene were two Spitfire squadrons from Douglas Bader's 'Duxford Wing', together with a Hurricane squadron from North Weald. The German bombers and their Bf.109 escorts faced a tough retreat. The RAF fighters harried and pressed the Luftwaffe back across the Channel; many losses were taken on both sides. But that night the bombers came again. Their target was easy to find: the fires caused by that afternoon's incendiaries were still blazing like beacons over east London.

'London's burning,' Göring told his wife over the telephone that night, gloating at the day's success.

What Göring did not know was that Dowding, Park and the rest of Fighter Command were unspeakably grateful to him for his change of direction. If the Luftwaffe had continued its raids on RAF bases for just a few days more, Fighter Command would effectively have abandoned the south of England.

Gegen London
Air Operations 7–14 September

7 September. Göring took personal command of his Luftwaffe for the first great raid on London and took up position on Cap Gris Nez to watch the armada. Every available aircraft was thrown into the attack which began in the late afternoon. The British squadrons were positioned to counter another attack on the airfields. Only too late was it realized that the target was London. Fires were started which acted as beacons for the night attack. When the dead were counted, 306 Londoners had been killed. Losses: RAF — 25 aircraft and 16 pilots; Luftwaffe — 41 aircraft and 52 aircrew.

8 September. Both sides rested, or licked their wounds, and there was little activity.

9 September. The Luftwaffe attempted a return to London, but this time Fighter Command was waiting and turned back the bombers. At night, however, the bombers found their target and a further 412 Londoners were killed. Losses: RAF — 17 aircraft and 6 pilots; Luftwaffe — 30 aircraft and 38 aircrew.

10–14 September. Few aircraft ventured over Britain in the daylight, but London was bombed at night. Bad weather with rain helped discourage the Luftwaffe from making further attacks.

Night attacks, guided by the fires lit from previous raids, continued for forty-three consecutive nights, except for 14 November 1940, when the Luftwaffe attacked and destroyed the centre of Coventry. On the 15th they returned to London, but in reduced concentrations as the attacks spread to other cities. Over a thousand Londoners had died, and many thousands more were injured or homeless, but the sacrifice saved the RAF.

Battle of the Barges

All over Britain, last minute preparations were being made to repel the invasion. Troops were moved to the south of the country, along with tanks and heavy guns. The Home Guard and Civil Defence were alerted. Hitler had even issued an open warning. On 4 September, addressing a public assembly at the Sportplatz in Berlin, he earned hysterical applause for his stated intention to 'erase' British cities. 'In England,' he said, 'they keep asking, "Why doesn't he come?" Be calm, be calm. He is coming!' On the 6th, British Chiefs of Staff issued a Stage 2 Alert, a formal warning that the invasion could be expected 'within the next three days'. The final alert would be codenamed 'Cromwell', meaning that the invasion was imminent.

Long before now, British intelligence had started reporting movements of shipping, large and small, on the inland waterways of Germany and the occupied countries. It was clear that a vast and motley invasion fleet was being assembled, slowly converging on the Channel ports. Specially converted, unarmed Spitfires flew risky photographic missions to monitor the daily build-up. The top-secret Ultra code-breaker machine was furnishing corroborative evidence. Everything pointed to the Wehrmacht troops crossing the Dover Straits in huge concentrations, at any moment.

And indeed, on 30 August, General von Brauchitsch, as commander-in-chief of Hitler's Army High Command, had completed his plan for Operation Sealion. As soon as the Luftwaffe had achieved air superiority, the Kriegsmarine would lay out protected corridors across the Channel and the Wehrmacht landing forces would establish two main bridgeheads between Folkestone and Worthing. The date and timing of the invasion would depend on the Führer's orders and the weather.

On 7 September the British Combined Intelligence Committee concluded that the invasion was about to begin. The weather was fine. The tide was favourable. That afternoon the Committee passed its recommendations to the Chiefs of Staff, who sat down to debate them just as the first raids began on London. In some confusion, the signal was given: 'Cromwell'. All over southern England, while bombs rained down on London, Civil Defence and Home Guard units went to battle stations, and church bells were rung, the agreed sign of invasion.

The following day, as results of the Luftwaffe raids were assessed and the confusion over 'Cromwell' was cleared up, a few red faces were dismissed as unimportant beside the loss of life in London and the heavy casualties taken by Fighter Command (twenty-eight, to the Luftwaffe's forty-one). But, to the bewilderment of British planners, the invasion fleet had not moved. What was Hitler waiting for? Speculation was pointless; action was required. To forestall the expected enemy move, Bomber Command was authorized to attack the fleet while it still lay in Channel ports and creeks.

Air Chief Marshal Portal's bombers had already made minor and sporadic raids over industrial and military targets in Germany and the occupied countries. Now they would concentrate on destroying the armada of naval vessels, requisitioned trawlers, tugs and barges as it converged on the coastal embarkation points. A regular nightly routine was established, with Blenheims and Beauforts attacking low from the sea, while Whitleys and Hampdens droned in to drop their bombload over the packed basins and harbours of Calais, Dunkirk, Boulogne. Finding the harbours was not difficult, but hitting a worthwhile target was a different matter. It was impossible to be accurate enough to select individual vessels or even groups of ships. Bombs were aimed in the general direction of the targets and the rest was left to luck in the hope that the bombs did not fall wide and kill French civilians.

This low-key series of attacks continued over the next fortnight. There were no dramatic results, but 'The Battle of the Barges', as it became known, would help to persuade Hitler the invasion must be called off.

Barging Back

The fleet for the invasion force had been assembled by 4 September. 168 transport ships totalling 704,548 tons, 1910 barges, 419 tugs and trawlers, and 1600 motorboats had been assembled in just six weeks.

The German Naval Staff announced that they would be ready to cross the Channel on the 19th, but needed ten days' notice to sweep for mines and make final preparations. The earliest day that the landing could take place (due to the tides) was 21 September; the ideal day was the 24th and the latest was the 27th. Hitler would therefore have to make a decision around 11 September, but he delayed until the 14th and then waited three more days, which meant that he missed the tides.

The next date when moon and tides would be favourable was 8 October, but by that time it was clear that air superiority had not been won.

Bomber Command had been ordered on 4 July to pay special attention to the invasion fleet, but during the whole of July only 66 tons of bombs had been dropped on the barges. This had little effect! The most effective attack was made on the Dortmund–Ems canal on 12 August which blocked it for ten days.

In July and August Bomber Command made 1,097 sorties against airfields and the fleet and lost 61 aircraft. As the fleet grew so did the attacks. In September over 1,000 tons of bombs were dropped on the fleet. The total number of barges sunk was 214, over one-tenth of the fleet.

London Takes It

If the worst of the agony was over for the RAF's airfields and sector stations, it was only just beginning for the capital. From teatime on 7 September 1940 until May the following year, almost without interruption, Londoners were subjected to the worst that the Luftwaffe could throw at them. It was the start of the London 'blitz' — the German word having undergone a radical translation in crossing the English Channel. The threat of invasion had by no means passed, but the Battle of Britain had entered a whole new phase.

It began with the night war. Although the Luftwaffe bombers arrived over London in the hours of daylight too, the most concerted attacks, which would continue until early November, were always made under cover of night. The long-range bombers — He.111s and Ju.88s — from Stumpff's Luftflotte 5 in Norway and Denmark had been brought south to bolster the already considerable might of Kesselring and Sperrle. The Stukas and the vulnerable Me.110s were held back to provide short-range cover across the Dover Straits. Otherwise, every serviceable aircraft in Luftflotten 2 and 3 was to fly every possible night.

The first night was 7 September, a resumption of the afternoon's savagery. Guided by the glow of fires still blazing from their earlier visitation, Göring's bombers returned to blast the East End and the City. The RAF's fighters, handicapped by the dark, were like blind men feeling their way across the sky. London's ground defences, idle for so long, thundered into action at last, while searchlights stiffly probed the night. AA Command was already rushing extra guns into London, but in vain; they contributed more noise than damage to the enemy.

On the 8th the massed bombers returned, after a quiet day, for a busy night's work over London. On the 9th they came in even greater numbers; again on the 10th, despite cloud and intermittent rain. And so it would go on, night after night. Occasionally the bombers risked a daylight raid, and then watchers on the streets of London could observe the high-altitude vapour trails that marked the progress of each savage dogfight. More often office workers would wake after an uncomfortable night in shelters, then wearily pick their way to central London through rubble and disrupted rail and bus services.

Every night the sirens wailed as dusk fell and the raiders returned. Every night, millions of Londoners slept in Anderson shelters in the back garden, or Morrison shelters in the basement; or joined hundreds of others in community shelters or on the platforms of Underground stations. Up above, the newly co-ordinated fire brigades and Civil Defence volunteers fought multiple infernos. Bells clanging, emergency vehicles sped through streets laced with canvas hoses and lit by flames. Homes, shops, businesses were demolished. Men, women and children were killed. Every day the survivors woke to further tragedies and devastation. But Hitler would not have the pleasure of watching Londoners submit. If only to spite that raving madman in Berlin, London could take it.

For the first time the British man in the street was in the 'Front Line', and not only men but women and children, babes to pensioners. Such was the confusion of the times that it proved impossible to compile accurate lists of the dead and injured. In some cases dozens of people died in a single incident, buried in rubble or burned beyond recognition. It took months to verify the number of casualties. In other cases a person reported missing would turn up later unharmed after going away for a few days.

From the outbreak of war to 6 September 1940 (the day before the first 'Blitz' on London) 257 people were killed in the capital and 1441 elsewhere in Britain. By the end of 1940 that total had risen to 22,069 of which 13,339 were Londoners.

A particularly tragic incident happened on the night of 13 October 1940. The air rad sirens had sent Londoners down to the shelters once more and at Public Shelter No. 5, the basement of a block of flats in Stoke Newington, a large number of people took cover. What is thought to have been a single, very large bomb scored a direct hit on the five-storey block and penentrated into the basement before exploding. In an instant all five floors collapsed on top of the people in the basement. Every exit was blocked by hundreds of tons of rubble. The explosion had also severed gas, water and sewage pipes. Raw effluent and water flooded into the basement. Even as rescue teams struggled through the masonry and choking dust, the survivors entombed below were drowning as water filled the basement. It took eleven days for rescue parties to recover the bodies. When work was completed 154 bodies had been recovered, twenty-six of which defied identification.

As senior échelons of the RAF were beginning to suspect, the Luftwaffe had lost sight of its main objective: to achieve air superiority prior to an invasion. But still the threat persisted, despite Bomber Command's continuing efforts to sink the German invasion fleet: on the night of 12 September a total of eighty barges were sunk in Ostend alone. However, hundreds more tugs and lighters were arriving through the Dutch and French canals. Apparently, the invasion would go ahead.

The Ides of September

The unrestrained bombing of London marked a decisive point in the course of the Battle of Britain and set a pattern for the raids of the next few days. On 9 September a large raid was broken up and bombs were scattered all over the southern outskirts of London. On the 11th, another large-scale attack was defeated before significant damage could be caused to the capital. A pattern now seemed to be developing of raids on alternate days, for the 12th was a quiet day with rain and cloud. This continued into the next day when several small raids were launched against London. No significant attack developed on the 14th, so would the pattern repeat itself with a heavy raid on the 15th? This was the question hanging in the air when Churchill arrived at 11 Group's HQ at 11 o'clock that morning. As Park escorted the Prime Minister into the operations room the answer lay before them on the plotting table, for reports from RDF stations had sent WAAF plotters into action and markers were being assembled like the pieces of a chess game. A large force of aircraft had been detected massing near Calais. It seemed all too likely that the formation would soon set course across the Channel.

At 1105 hours Park made his opening gambit: Nos. 72 and 92 Squadrons were to scramble from Biggin Hill to patrol Canterbury at 25,000 feet. Ten minutes later eight more squadrons were airborne, followed by four more squadrons at 1120.

The enemy still hadn't crossed the coast, but undoubtedly they were coming. Leigh-Mallory's 'Big Wing' of 12 Group had now had time to assemble and climb to combat height; thus at 1125 hours the five squadrons of the Duxford Wing were ordered up to patrol Hornchurch at 25,000 feet.

Shortly after half past eleven three columns of Dorniers, escorted by their Messerschmitt bodyguard, crossed the Kent coast between Dover and Ramsgate. Within minutes the two Spitfire squadrons from Biggin Hill joined combat with the escort. No. 603 Squadron then made an attempt to distract the Me.109s and lead them away, but most of the German pilots stuck grimly by the bombers. Over Maidstone two Hurricane squadrons met the Dorniers head-on and claimed three of the bombers destroyed.

As this combat was being fought, six further squadrons were ordered up. The enemy formation meanwhile struggled on. At 1205 hours the lead bombers were over London, and so were nine fighter squadrons.

One of the Dorniers was being flown by Oberleutnant Robert Zehbe, a twenty-seven year old pilot with the bomber unit *Kampfgeschwader 76*. One of his machine's engines had been giving trouble and when he reached London he had fallen behind his comrades. Then the inevitable happened, as one after the other Hurricanes and Spitfires queued up to down this lame duck. By now the bomber was in a bad way and the port engine was in flames. As the bomber lost height two men baled out. The wing was well alight, but still the fighters came. Zehbe at last had to bale out himself, leaving his young gunner already dead behind his gun. Finally the Dornier broke up into pieces and crashed to earth around Victoria Station in the centre of London. One wing came away and struck the Hurricane being flown by Sergeant Ray Holmes and he also took to his parachute. This action was seen by thousands of Londoners and so an epic story of the battle was born.

By 1220 hours the last bombers had left London, but even as they fled four more fighter squadrons harried them all the way to the coast. The wreckage of six Dornier Do.17s and seven Me.109s was found scattered over southeast England.

The Gauntlet

No sooner had the pilots recovered from the morning's combat than RDF plots again began to indicate a build-up of aircraft in the Calais–Boulogne area. The first reports came in at 1345 and within minutes twelve fighter squadrons had been scrambled. At 1205 three forces were plotted moving across the Channel towards Dungeness and Dover. Ten minutes later three parallel columns of Heinkel He.111s and Dornier Do.17s reached Maidstone on a front thirty miles wide. This force of around 150 bombers was rapidly being overtaken by several smaller formations of Bf.109s coming up from behind. A further fourteen fighter squadrons, including the Duxford Wing, were now airborne, making a total of twenty-six squadrons in all.

This, then, is the popular impression of the Battle of Britain. A wall of bombers escorted by hordes of shepherding Messerschmitts stretching as far as the eye could see and all this set against a backdrop of puffy white clouds floating in a blue sky. Facing this seemingly invincible armada were 'The Few', isolated and outnumbered in the cockpits of their Hurricanes and Spitfires.

The first pilots to engage the enemy were from 222 and 603 Squadrons, but before they could attack the bombers the Bf.109s pounced and two Spitfires were shot down. Squadron Leader Denholm baled out, but twenty-two-year-old Flying Officer Arthur Pease, son of Sir Richard Pease of Richmond, Yorkshire, died when his aircraft crashed. Heroic though their efforts were, the British pilots were brushed aside by sheer weight of numbers and the armada forged onwards. 73 Squadron had lost one of its pilots in the morning's battle and fielded just five Hurricanes, but it was

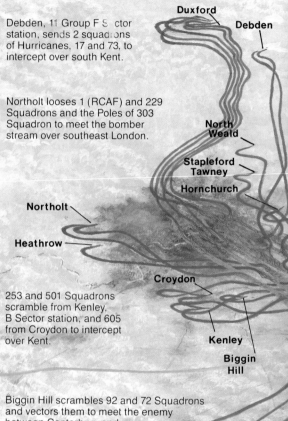

Park requests support from 12 Group through Fighter Command Headquarters. Air Vice-Marshal Sir Trafford Leigh-Mallory, AOC-in-C 12 Group, scrambles the Duxford Wing, now comprising 5 squadrons: 19, 242, 302, 310 and 611. Douglas Bader leads them south over London to intercept.

Debden, 11 Group F Sector station, sends 2 squadrons of Hurricanes, 17 and 73, to intercept over south Kent.

Northolt looses 1 (RCAF) and 229 Squadrons and the Poles of 303 Squadron to meet the bomber stream over southeast London.

253 and 501 Squadrons scramble from Kenley, B Sector station, and 605 from Croydon to intercept over Kent.

Duxford

Debden

North Weald

Stapleford Tawney

Hornchurch

Northolt

Heathrow

Croydon

Kenley

Biggin Hill

Middle Wallop

Help is requested from Air Vice-Marshal Sir Quintin Brand, AOC-in-C 10 Group, to patrol over Portsmouth and the Solent in the absence of Sector A aircraft from Tangmere and Westhampnett. He sends 609 Squadron from Middle Wallop.

Biggin Hill scrambles 92 and 72 Squadrons and vectors them to meet the enemy between Canterbury and Dungeness.

Westhampnett

Tangmere

Brighton

Portsmouth

During the afternoon raid, Squadrons 607, 213 and 602, controlled by A Sector at Tangmere, are scrambled and ordered to fly across the south of England to meet the attackers.

11 Group E Sector contributes 504 Squadron from Hendon, controlled from North Weald, while B Flight of 257 Squadron flies south from Martlesham Heath. They meet the enemy over Maidstone, some having attained an altitude of 19,000ft (5,850m).

Martlesham Heath

During the heat of the battle, control often crossed sector lines drawn on the operations table. Thus, Hornchurch controlled 222 and 603 Squadrons from its home base, and also 41 operating from Rochester. They were all scrambled early to meet the raid over Kent.

Rochford

Gravesend

Eastchurch

West Malling

Biggin Hill, C Sector station, controlled 72 Squadron from its base and 66 from Gravesend. All were scrambled early and met the enemy over Kent.

Eastbourne

Enemy movements include a number of flights over the Channel and wandering inland, tracked by radar and the Observer Corps — probably reconnaissance probes and rescue seaplanes. The Luftwaffe made few feints or diversions, but as these tracks might have been hostile bombers they were plotted on operations-room tables.

they who approached next. One pilot reported seeing fifty bombers escorted by fifty Bf.110s, twenty times their own number, but into the attack they went. Later they claimed to have damaged three bombers and escaped themselves without loss.

Thus far the enemy formation had met little serious opposition, but as the leaders approached the suburbs of southeast London, Fighter Command attacked with Nos. 66, 72, 504, 249, 17, 257, 605, 501, 92, 41 and the five squadrons of Bader's Duxford Wing — Nos. 242, 19, 302, 310 and 611.

One of the Hurricane pilots with 605 Squadron was Flying Officer Cooper-Slipper. He came in close to make an attack on a Dornier of *Kampfgeschwader 3* over Marden in Kent, but misjudged his approach and crashed into the bomber. His port wing was torn off and he was lucky to get out before his plane crashed. All four men in the Dornier baled out, but one was killed when his parachute failed to open fully before he hit the ground.

British Chain Home radar could see well into France, and could thus follow the build-up of the raid. Chain Home Low watched out for surprise low-level raids, which did not occur.

Dunkirk

Pas-de-Calais

Luftwaffe bombers, mainly Ju.88s, Do.17 and He.111s, took off from over 20 airfields. They climbed to rendez-vous above the Pas de Calais, the first arriving in British CH radar range at about 1030. The first moves towards London were plotted at about 1050.

Bf.109 fighters took off last, climbing fast to catch up with the bombers they had to escort as their range was limited. Despite this, many had to turn back, and a number ran out of fuel before reaching home.

September Flames

As the first aircraft were beginning to drop their bombs over London, another smaller formation was detected further south. 213 and 607 Squadrons from Tangmere were ordered to intercept and found the intruders over the borders of Kent and Surrey. Unbelievably this formation was as big as one of those already over London, another eighty bombers, but without a fighter escort as they were apparently hoping to sneak in behind the main raid. Twenty-four year old Pilot Officer Patrick Stephenson made a head-on attack against a Dornier, but struck his foe and was forced to bale out. The bomber dived straight into the ground where its bomb-load exploded with such violence that hardly anything was left of the crew to bury.

All available fighters were now engaged. Over Tunbridge Wells No. 1 Squadron Royal Canadian Air Force was in action. Flying Officer Arthur Nesbitt from Montreal baled out and Arthur Yuile was wounded in the shoulder. Ross Smither from Ontario was killed. Sergeant Potter from 19 Squadron chased some returning aircraft over the Channel and crashed into the sea off the French coast — he was rescued by the Germans and spent the rest of the war in a prison camp. Sub-Lieutenant Richard Cork, on detachment to 242 Squadron from the Fleet Air Arm, claimed the destruction of two Dorniers before he was attacked by Bf.109s. Bullets riddled his Hurricane, but he managed to make an emergency landing and escaped unhurt. From the Polish 302 Squadron, Flight Lieutenant Tadeusz Chlopik attacked a Dornier and was then shot down. He attempted to bale out, but fell with an unopened parachute. Two Czechoslovakian pilots from 310 Squadron were shot down over Essex and both baled out safely. Flying Officer Michael Jebb of 504 Squadron was shot down near Dartford and was terribly burnt — he died four days later.

The many sacrifices of this day, however, did not pass unavenged for the German losses were also high. *Kampfgeschwader 2* lost eight Dorniers. One was so badly damaged that it was forced to land with both its engines stopped. Another crew baled out over Chatham and their aircraft dived into a street, while a third crashed into a Kent field taking three of its crew with it. The remaining five aircraft all crashed into the sea.

The other Dornier unit in the afternoon raid, *Kampfgeschwader 3*, lost six aircraft. From Leutnant Dumler's crew only one man managed to get out before his aircraft dived into a street in Essex. All of Leutnant Michaelis's crew baled out, but one's parachute failed and another was so badly injured that he died in hospital. One pilot made a successful forced landing on the Isle of Grain and two more bombers exploded when they crashed. The sixth Dornier had its port engine set on fire over London and it crashed into the Thames Estuary.

In addition to the Dorniers, Heinkel He.111s of *Kampfgeschwader 26* and *Kampfgeschwader 53* were in action. Only one KG26 machine was lost but KG53 lost six aircraft. One came down at the Woolwich Arsenal and landed safely, but before its four crew could get out its bombs exploded and they were killed. Three crews were luckier for they crash-landed their Heinkels safely. Major Gruber was the commanding officer of II/KG53 and was flying as sixth man in aircraft A1+GM. They were attacked by Spitfires of 92 Squadron over Kent after having already been hit in the port engine by anti-aircraft fire. One of the gunners, Feldwebel Andreas Grassl, was killed by bullets and was left behind when the other five baled out. The bomber then disintegrated in the air.

Nor was it just the bombers which suffered, for at least six Bf.109s were shot down in the afternoon raid.

As the Luftwaffe retired to the east, along the Thames Estuary, the Poles of 303 Squadron attacked. Those that chose to retire southwestwards were met by 602 and 238 Squadrons.

Flying with the fanatical determination that the Polish fighter pilots were renowned for, 303 Squadron

pressed home its attack. Nineteen-year old Sergeant Andruszkow attacked and damaged a Dornier, but was then shot down by Bf.109s. He baled out safely. Fellow countryman Michal Brzezowski was also shot down in the same engagement, but he was less fortunate and crashed into the Thames Estuary. Neither he nor his machine were ever found. Six other pilots, including their British squadron leader, Ronald Kellett, limped back to Northolt with their damaged Hurricanes.

The bombs which fell on London were dropped between 1445 and 1515 hours. At Dartford a power station received three direct hits. At East Ham a telephone exchange was put out of action and a gas holder destroyed. In all, more destruction resulted from the afternoon raid than from the morning's, but this was still small compared to the damage done on 7 September when three times the tonnage of bombs was dropped. The casualty figures as officially stated were: London, 52 people killed and 153 injured; elsewhere, another ten people killed. The real figure, however, was probably greater than this.

September's Embers

The second half of September saw a slight
reduction in the scale of Luftwaffe activity and few
of the slow Dorniers and Heinkels were dispatched.
Instead greater numbers of fast Ju.88s were
employed along with Bf.110s and of course the ever
present Bf.109s. On 18 September III/KG77, a
Ju.88 unit which had only recently been brought
into the front line, lost nine aircraft on a single raid.

The next big day was 27 September, when fine
weather tempted an increase in the tempo of activity.

The day's activity began just after 0800 with a raid
by Bf.110s and Bf.109s that seemed to cavort over
Surrey and Sussex aimlessly. The reason for this
action became clear shortly after when a large
formation of Ju.88s appeared, but the German plan
was going wrong. The first raid brought Fighter
Command into action and as soon as they had
landed, the Ju.88s should have raced to London.
Unfortunately the Ju.88s were behind schedule and
missed their rendezvous with a Bf.109 escort,
giving the British fighters time to re-arm and refuel.
In spite of frantic calls for assistance twelve Ju.88s
from I and II Gruppen KG77 were shot down.
When Bf.109s eventually appeared on the scene
over Surrey savage dogfights developed. Hurricanes
from 303 and 501 Squadrons were involved along

with Spitfires from 92 Squadron. Flight Sergeant Sidney went down with his Spitfire and crashed into the garden of a large house in Walton-on-Thames. Flying Officer Zak, a Pole with 303 Squadron, baled out of his Hurricane when it was set alight over Leatherhead. Sergeant Andruszkow had safely baled out of a Hurricane on 15 September but on this day his luck ran out and he went down with his plane. Sergeant Victor Ekins escaped with slight burns as his Hurricane caught fire when he was shot down by a Bf.110. To offset the Allied losses, seven Bf.110s of Lehrgeschwader I were lost in combat over Surrey and Sussex.

No sooner had the London raid departed than the action switched to the West Country where a raid was attempted on Bristol. This raid was spearheaded by nineteen Bf.110s of *Erprobungsgruppe 210* escorted by twenty-seven Bf.110s of III/ZG26 and followed by thirty He.111s of KG55. Five squadrons from 10 Group met the raid and turned back all but the leading Bf.110s. *Erprobungsgruppe 210* lost four and III/ZG26 three Bf.110s. Only KG55 escaped without loss.

---

15 September — Fact and Propaganda

Figures released in 1940 by the RAF:

Enemy bombers destroyed	125
Enemy fighters destroyed	47
Enemy aircraft damaged	11
Total:	183
RAF losses	23

With fifty years of hindsight, the real figures can now be assessed:

Luftwaffe bombers destroyed	29
Luftwaffe fighters destroyed	23
Total destroyed:	52
Luftwaffe bombers damaged	19
Luftwaffe fighters damaged	6
Total damaged:	25
RAF fighters destroyed	27
RAF fighters damaged	25
RAF pilots killed	13
RAF pilots injured	12

Although two Luftwaffe aircraft were lost for every one RAF fighter, it is purely on the strength of the original exaggerated figures that 15 September has been observed as a day symbolic of the achievement of Fighter Command.

Into Autumn

28 September. Another attempted attack on London beaten off. Churchill sent a message: 'Pray congratulate Fighter Command on the results of yesterday. The scale and intensity of the fighting and the heavy losses of the enemy make 27th September rank with 15th September and 15th August, as the third great and victorious day of the Fighter Command during the course of the Battle of Britain.'
29–30 September. September ended with daylight raids costing the RAF 41 lost. Luftwaffe losses: 59. Although 15 September set the seal on the invasion, the big battle of 27 September finished the Luftwaffe's belief in its ability to break the RAF's defence of Britain. And the irony was that now, when it was too late, the weather improved into an Indian summer. Despite Göring's unabated optimism, RAF fighters were coming up in undiminished numbers, even if their pilots were, by now, almost too tired and strained to achieve the best results. Equally weary Luftwaffe crews began to find more cost-effective ways to continue the battle. Although the night raids continued, sometimes using electronic aids to bomb through cloud and darkness, the use of bombers during the day was too costly. The vulnerable Stukas had been totally withdrawn and by now, even the previous vaunted Bf.110s were being escorted by 109s unless they could use cloud to sneak in unseen. Göring had even ordered that only one officer should fly with each bomber to save valuable lives.
1 October. Bf.110s carrying bombs slung on under-wing racks, escorted by Bf.109s, raided London, Southampton and Portsmouth. At night, Luftflotte 3's bombers attacked London, Liverpool and Manchester.
2–6 October. Changeable and generally cloudy weather restricted operations. The majority of aircraft over Britain were fighters, the bombers now restricted to night raids. RAF losses: 14. Luftwaffe losses: 53.
7 October. Much improved weather prompted a continuous stream of fighter-bombers to cross southeastern England. In the West Country an attack on Yeovil led to the loss of eight Bf.110s. RAF losses: 4. Luftwaffe losses: 14.
8–14 October. The new Luftwaffe tactic of sending small groups of fast, bomb-carrying Bf.109s towards London kept Fighter Command fully stretched.
12 October. Faced with a loss of 215 barges and invasion transports to Bomber Command, Hitler ordered the fleet to disperse. The Battle of Britain had thus been won. RAF losses: 26. Luftwaffe losses: 46.
15 October. Heavy raids on London by day and night resulted in 262 dead and heavy damage to property.
16–31 October. Attacks fell into a distinct routine: Bf.109 *Jabo* fighter-bombers by day and Luftflotte 3 bombers against London and major cities by night.

By 31 October, the Luftwaffe had lost over 2600 airmen killed and 950 taken prisoner. Britain had lost 415 pilots.

Autumn Missed

There can be little doubt that the air battles of 15 September came as a shock to the Luftwaffe High Command, for their intelligence sources had indicated that Fighter Command had been depleted in both aircraft and pilots. They had suffered heavy losses in France, over the Channel, and now over England itself. According to Luftwaffe intelligence there should not have been any significant number of fighters left to challenge them. Clearly they had been wrong and a change in tactics was urgently called for if their bomber force was not to be eliminated.

On 17 September Hitler postponed Operation *Seelöwe* indefinitely as it stood no chance of success so long as the RAF maintained control of the air space around Britain. Göring, in spite of all his boasts, had failed to gain any measure of air superiority; in fact there was precious little to show in return for the expenditure of so many men and machines.

In the final half of September, and thereafter, attention was focused on the bombing of towns and cities and the new German tactics sought to exploit the weakest points in Britain's defences.

In the previous weeks Bf.109s had been fitted with bomb racks to carry a single 250kg bomb under the centre-line of the fuselage and these were allotted to specialist 'Jabo' *Staffeln*. 'Jabo' was an abbreviation for *Jagdbomber* (fighter-bomber) and the aircraft usually had solid triangles painted on their sides. The tactics had been developed by the experimental group *Erprobungsgruppe 210* and involved flying either fast and low, or at great height. If the Messerschmitts crossed the coast low then the defences had little warning and found the raiders hard to catch. If the Jabos came in very high then the Spitfires and Hurricanes did not have time to climb to their height and if they did they were out-classed by the Bf.109s which had a better performance at altitude. Both of these tactics began to stretch Fighter Command and its pilots to the limit.

The Germans had learned a costly lesson — that twin-engined bombers could not survive in daylight against single-engined fighters. Now the Heinkels, Dorniers and Junker 88s would be sent out under cover of darkness. The British defences were almost helpless at night, but the Luftwaffe were remarkably well-equipped for the role. A specialist bomber group (*Kampfgruppe 100*) had been flying specially equipped Heinkels over Britain for several months and had perfected the technique of radio navigation to a point where a high degree of accuracy could be achieved. It was also possible for ordinary bombers to fly along a corridor marked by radio signals using their standard equipment. Against this well-organized and practised force stood six Blenheim and two Defiant squadrons. However, the Blenheims were too slow to catch some bombers and the Defiants were only pressed into service after their failure in daylight; neither had reliable airborne interception equipment. Some Spitfire and Hurricane squadrons took part in 'Cat's Eye' patrols, but successes were few as they relied mainly on luck to find a bomber. It was only with the introduction of the Bristol Beaufighter early in 1944 that the night defence of Britain became effective and German bomber losses began to rise again, but by this time the most devastating raids had already taken place.

On the night of 14–15 November 1940, Coventry

was selected as the target for a concentrated raid. *Kampfgruppe 100*'s Heinkels led the raid and dropped over 10,000 incendiary bombs which started the fires that drew another 400 bombers to the city. 554 people were killed and 865 seriously injured. Only one aircraft was lost, and that was shot down by anti-aircraft fire. Although this raid was, and still is, seen as an act of wanton and senseless destruction it was in fact another example of retaliation. On the night of 8 November, RAF Bomber Command had executed a damaging raid on Munich, the very day that Hitler was to make a speech in that city. It was an important event for Hitler and the Nazi Party as it came on the eve of the commemoration of the Munich Putsch (9 November 1923). Hitler was enraged by the bombing and ordered a revenge attack. Coventry was an important manufacturing centre for the war effort and as such was seen as a legitimate target, but the bombing of Coventry was another step in the war's escalation.

Over the next six months every major town, city and port in Britain was bombed, with horrendous loss of life and damage to property. London was bombed almost every night and on the night of 10 May 1941, the capital suffered its greatest ordeal. The moon was full and, the Thames drained by an ebb tide, conditions were ideal for a fire raid. The Luftwaffe crews made 570 sorties, some crews making two or even three missions that night, and dropping hundreds of bombs and tens of thousands of incendiaries. London burnt, and with low tide in the Thames, the firemen were unable to contain the fires, which spread out of control. Over 1,000 Londoners were killed and thousands more injured. The era of total war had arrived in all its horror.

In The Dark

On the first day of October, Dowding's group commanders were reviewing the previous day's events. Park's fighters had intercepted the attempted raid on London, while Brand's 10 Group had put up five squadrons to counter the Luftwaffe plans for Yeovil. The outcome had been terrible for the raiders: nearly fifty aircraft lost. But in their desperation the Luftwaffe commanders were obviously casting round for new ways to penetrate the RAF's aerial screen, and at Fighter Command the British tacticians were trying to keep one step ahead. The enemy had changed his objectives from the airbases to the cities, had started night bombing, had substantially increased the fighter escort protecting each formation of bombers, had begun to use converted fighter-bombers in fast, small-scale attacks, and furthermore had learned sophisticated deception techniques — such as sending up large, high-altitude formations of fighters to lure the Hurricanes and Spitfires away from a bombing raid, or letting a single Messerschmitt amble temptingly across the sky, apparently alone, then suddenly pouncing from on high when the unwary RAF pilot went in for the kill. The likelihood was that Kesselring and Sperrle were even now planning yet another new and disconcerting move.

Across the Channel, the Luftwaffe commanders were, indeed, engaged in urgent reconsideration. The losses of the previous day must never happen again, they agreed, so daylight bombing raids would be stopped. The Stukas had already been withdrawn, and the Bf.110s too; the converted 109s were proving a great success, but their single 250kg bomb was insufficient for the wholesale devastation Göring had ordered for British cities. The only solution was to step up the night offensive.

Ever since late August, regular nightly bombing raids had been made on ports, docks, industry and rail communications: London, Merseyside and the Midlands had been worst hit. The results were less devastating than some of the German pilots supposed; but they were certainly right in concluding that night interception was not one of the RAF's strengths. Dowding's pilots were flying blind; but the Luftwaffe had a remarkably accurate audible guide towards their target, provided by intersecting radio beams. German scientists had devised a radio navigation system, code-named *Knickebein* (literally 'crooked leg'), based on the Lorenz blind-landing aid in which two distinct radio transmissions — one of dots, the other dashes — were overlapped to provide a narrow continuous signal; by flying his aircraft along the line of the continuous signal, a pilot was enabled to land at night or in fog.

By a combination of luck and skill, the brilliant young R. V. Jones and his colleagues in scientific intelligence had discovered the existence of *Knickebein*; it then seemed simple enough to jam the beams. However, the Germans had taken a further step ahead, developing *X-Geraint*, an even more sophisticated combination of beams, which

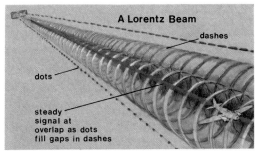

A Lorentz Beam

dashes

dots

steady
signal at
overlap as dots
fill gaps in dashes

first came into operation at the start of September 1940. *X-Geraint*, which was accurate to 50m at a range of 200 miles, was much harder to jam — in fact, the most effective counter-measure was to shoot down the aircraft following the beams.

But, until the RAF's airborne radar system was more reliable, the Spitfires and Hurricanes were unable to intercept the night raiders. Throughout October, with the longer nights marking the onset of winter, Fighter Command kept up vigorous daily

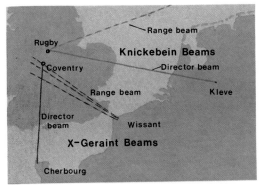

Range beam

Rugby

Knickebein Beams

Coventry

Director beam

Range beam

Kleve

Director
beam

Wissant

X-Geraint Beams

Cherbourg

patrols to deter the fighter-bombers, and with notable success. After dusk, however, the RAF's frustration was total.

As the new year dawned, however, the first generation of AI radar, albeit primitive, was fitted into Defiants and Blenheims. Due to problems of ground control and short range, success was limited. But soon improved sets were fitted into better aircraft: with practice and experience RAF night-fighter crews began to catch and destroy the Luftwaffe night bombers.

Night Fighters

Boulton Paul Defiant
Both 141 and 264 Squadrons, which had been given short shrift by Bf.109s, began to develop night fighting tactics in late 1940. The Defiant proved to be, if not good, at least a reasonable night fighter. It made a stable gun platform and its pilot could concentrate on flying, leaving the gunner to search for the enemy and open fire. Maximum speed 304mph. Armament — 4 machine guns.

Bristol Beaufighter
This was intended to be a long-range fighter and first flew in 1939. It was rushed into service by late 1940 and was the best night fighter available. It was also the only aircraft that could carry the heavy Airborne Interception radar. Maximum speed 323mph. Armament — four 20mm cannon and 6 machine guns.

Junkers Ju.88C
This aircraft appeared in 1940 but it was not until 1942 that 'Lichtenstein' airborne radar was developed and fitted. Maximum speed 298mph. Armament — three 20mm cannon and 3 machine guns.

Post-Mortem

Hitler had finally, on 12 October, ordered that the invasion of Britain should be 'postponed' until the following spring — although, as history tells us, the project was never revived. In fact, he had already turned his mind to the east, and was now considering plans to invade the country of his erstwhile ally, the Soviet Union. He was at least realist enough to see that Britain could not be conquered by the methods that had taken mainland Europe by storm, and certainly not while the RAF retained air supremacy. In the four months that the Battle of Britain had lasted, the largest and best equipped and most experienced air force in the world had been held at bay by a force only half its size: Fighter Command had destroyed 1733 German aircraft, while the Luftwaffe had destroyed 915 British fighters.

It is a sad irony that the two men chiefly responsible for Fighter Command's success during the Battle should immediately afterwards have faced condemnation and eclipse. Dowding and Park, his protégé, were alike in their devotion to the service and perhaps shared the mistaken assumption that a leader does not need to keep looking over his own shoulder. Dowding, aloof in manner, sometimes impatient in speech, had already trodden on a few Whitehall toes before the war broke out. He had also seen fit to delegate responsibility to trusted subordinates, declining to interfere with their decisions so long as his general strategy was followed. Keith Park worked in much the same way. In the Uxbridge ops room, for example, he watched and listened to his controllers rather than telling them what to do; he trusted them, and they responded in kind.

As the heat of the battle faded, old resentments found new outlets. Within the service and around the corridors of power, voices were raised against both Dowding and Park — and the bulk of their complaint concerned the 'wing' controversy. Neither man had handled the controversy well, as they admitted later. Dowding was on record as believing that 'the squadron will always be the largest tactical unit which it will be practically expedient to employ', as he told the Air Ministry on 19 August 1939, and he never saw fit to change his mind. Park shared his views, and rejected the 'wing' proposal when Leigh-Mallory of 12 Group put it to him. As demonstrated by the 'Duxford Wing', led by the idea's author and champion, the legless hero Douglas Bader, three or

four squadrons would operate jointly, meeting mass attacks with massed defences. Undoubtedly Bader's wing had its successes; but Park was exasperated at the delay caused by the several squadrons forming up. Park's 11 Group squadrons could not afford to spend ten, fifteen, even twenty minutes assembling in a wing; being further forward than 12 Group, their primary aim was simply to get into the air as fast as possible. When, on two or three occasions, the Duxford Wing arrived too late to offer the help Park had requested from 12 Group, his exasperation boiled over into open criticism of Leigh-Mallory.

Leigh-Mallory and Bader now fought back, determined to justify their belief in the wing. Both had their supporters, including the MP Peter Macdonald, who also happened to be Bader's adjutant. Macdonald's influence resulted in an official meeting being arranged at the Air Ministry on 17 October, chaired by Air Vice-Marshal Sholto Douglas, Deputy Chief of the Air Staff, with the stated aim of discussing tactics. Dowding and Park were both summoned to attend, as was Leigh-Mallory; and somehow, for reasons never explained, Bader himself was present, a very junior officer amid such exalted company. Sholto Douglas invited

Park to express his views, then Leigh-Mallory, then Bader. The enthusiastic and impassioned Bader carried the day. The meeting concluded that the wing theory should be developed and expanded.

Park, especially, felt as if he had been on trial. But it was Dowding who took the initial brunt of condemnation; his retirement, now scheduled for late November, was upheld, though there are still some who maintain he was dismissed. His position at Fighter Command was taken by Sholto Douglas. In December, Park was posted to a training group while 11 Group went to Leigh-Mallory, free at last to unfurl his wings. Although Park's career flourished later in the war, including a spell in Malta where he repeated his Battle of Britain tactics to equally good effect, and despite his subsequent knighthood, many who had served under him felt bitterly resentful of the Air Ministry's failure to acknowledge his brilliant contribution to Fighter Command's success in 1940.

Dowding, too, in the eyes of his many supporters, would gain inadequate recognition for his leadership. In 1943 he was made a peer, becoming Lord Dowding of Bentley Priory, but he was never granted the rank of Marshal of the RAF that he might seem to have earned. Only in 1988, eighteen years after his death,

was a statue unveiled to his memory, outside St Clement Danes in London, the RAF's own church. It was the culmination of a long campaign by his former 'chicks', the most fitting tribute they could pay him, to raise an enduring public reminder of this man's contribution to his country's survival.

'The Few' — Aircrew of Fighter Command

These are the nationalities of the men who qualified for the campaign award, the Battle of Britain Clasp. To qualify for this award a man must have flown at least one sortie with a squadron deemed to have taken part in the Battle of Britain. British 2353, Polish 145, New Zealander 126, Canadian 97, Czech 87, Belgian 29, Australian 29, South African 22, Free French 13, Irish 9, American 11, Southern Rhodesian 3, Jamaican 1, Newfoundlander 1, Palestinian 1. Total: 2927.

The Squadrons with which they must have flown to be considered eligible were: 1, 1 (RCAF), 3, 17, 19, 23, 25, 29, 32, 41, 43, 46, 54, 56, 64, 65, 66, 72, 73, 74, 79, 85, 87, 92, 111, 141, 145, 151, 152, 213, 219, 222, 229, 232, 234, 235, 236, 238, 242, 245, 247, 248, 249, 253, 257, 263, 264, 266, 302, 303, 310, 312, 501, 504, 600, 601, 602, 603, 604, 605, 607, 609, 610, 611, 615, 616, 421 Flt. 422 Flt. FIU 804 FAA 808 FAA.

The Chianti Party

There was a curious postscript to the Battle of Britain, written by the Italian dictator, Mussolini. He and Hitler were partners in the Berlin–Rome 'axis': the expression was coined by Mussolini, a felicitous exception to his usual forgettable bombast. Even to Hitler, tarred with the same brush, Il Duce was prone to megalomania: for one thing, he considered himself the Führer's equal. On 4 October Hitler told Mussolini that only bad weather was hindering the Luftwaffe's progress in Britain, repeating Göring's claim that 'four or five good days' would give the German pilots supremacy. No doubt hoping to snatch a last-minute share of the glory, Mussolini thereupon pressed a contingent of Italian bombers and fighters on Luftflotte 2 in Belgium.

The Italian air force, the Regia Aeronautica, although the apple of Mussolini's eye, was relatively ill-equipped and its pilots poorly trained; it was certainly not prepared for the conditions prevailing in these northern latitudes. When the first Italian aircraft arrived in Belgium, their bright blue and green camouflage made them stand out like peacocks among the 'eagles'. Their initial contribution to the Battle was made on the night of 25 October, when sixteen Fiat BR.20 bombers joined a raid on the east coast port of Harwich. In the darkness and confusion, the identity of these raiders was not suspected. Four days later, however, in broad daylight, eastern Kent was treated to a fly-past of fifteen BR.20s escorted by seventy CR.42 fighters. The biplane fighters looked like relics from the First World War, and the astonished AA guncrews around Manston and Ramsgate were momentarily deterred from firing; as soon as they opened up, however, the Italians disappeared.

But the 'Chianti party', as Fighter Command started calling it, did not properly begin until 11 November. During the day, two Hurricane squadrons from North Weald were scrambled to meet a sizeable threat reported by radar off the Thames estuary. The Hurricane pilots could hardly believe their eyes. The raiders comprised ten BR.20s with an escort of forty CR.42s. Brave as they were, the Italians were outclassed. Twelve of their aircraft were shot down within minutes, for the loss of no Hurricanes.

Belatedly the Italians had learnt a lesson that their Luftwaffe friends ought to have shared: daylight bombing raids over Britain were suicidal. The fighters, however, returned to make offensive sweeps, despite frequent interception from Spitfires and Hurricanes, and the bombers regularly added their deadly cargo to the nightly blitz on British cities. The 'party' continued intermittently throughout the winter. But, by April 1941, the Italians' enthusiasm had faded. The survivors would soon return to a sunnier theatre of war — the Mediterranean. In numbers of aircraft, the Regia Aeronautica was actually superior to the RAF. Having had this drawn to their attention, the RAF now made repeated raids on Italian aircraft factories in an attempt to halt further production.

Mussolini's contribution to the Battle of Britain was negligible, and earned sneers from the British press; his pilots, however, fought gallantly and well, and earned their adversaries' admiration.

Meanwhile, Bomber Command had taken the war back across the Channel; as well as Luftwaffe airfields and industrial targets, regular bombing raids were reaching Berlin. Berliners were getting a taste of the same bitter medicine handed out to Londoners. Hitler was furious. He had acknowledged that a German invasion of Britain was now impossible, but he ordered Göring to step up the 'reprisal raids'. The London blitz, the non-stop onslaught that had begun in early September, had already caused terrible civilian casualties and turned whole districts into smouldering heaps of rubble; now it was the turn of other cities and coastal towns.

Every night that weather conditions allowed, the German bombers returned, following their radio navigation beams to Birmingham, Liverpool, Plymouth, Coventry... The devastation caused by incendiaries in Coventry on the night of 14 November 1940 was to become a benchmark against which other cities would measure their loss. These were no reprisal raids; this was savagery unleashed by a madman whose wishes had been thwarted. The Battle of Britain was over, but he would not give up.

Regia Aeronautica

Mussolini led Italy into the war on 10 June, when the Battle of France was all but won. In July, Il Duce offered to assist the Luftwaffe in their campaign against Britain, but his offer was politely turned down. Still keen to get into action, Mussolini was finally allowed to base some units in Belgium under the command of Luftflotte 2. The force was called the 'Corpo Aereo Italiano' and consisted of 80 Fiat BR.20 bombers (13th and 43rd Stormi), 50 Fiat CR.42 fighters (18th Gruppo) and 48 Fiat G.50 fighters (20th Gruppo) and a few CANT Z.1007Bis transports.

Fiat CR.42. A very manoeuvrable aircraft produced in 1939 and used in the Mediterranean until the Italian Armistice in 1943. Speed — 274mph. Range — 485 miles. Armament — 2 machine guns.

Fiat BR.20M. This bomber first appeared in late 1939 and like the CR.42 served until 1943. Speed — 267mph. Range — 1193 miles. Armament — 4 machine guns. Bomb load — 3550lbs.

Operations

25 October. Night raid on Harwich by 16 BR.20s. One crashed on take-off, two crews baled out on return when fuel was low.
29 October. Ramsgate. 15 bombers and 73 fighters — many returned with AA damage.
5 November. Night raid on Harwich by 8 BR.20s.
11 November. Daylight raid on Harwich by 10 BR.20s and 40 CR.42s.
17 November. Night raid on Harwich by 6 BR.20s.
20 November. Night raid on Harwich and Ipswich by 12 BR.20s.

Below: **Fiat G.50 Fighter**
First flown in 1937, the G.50 was one of the first Italian all-metal, single-seat, single-engined monoplane fighters. However, its under-powered engine and open cockpit made it outdated before WWII began. Had the Group sent to Belgium been used during the day, they would probably have fared worse than the CR.42 biplanes. **Engine:** 840hp Fiat 14-cylinder 2-row radial. **Dimensions:** Span 36' 1" (11m). Length 27' 2" (8.29m). **Weight:** 5511lb (2500kg) loaded. **Max. speed:** 302mph (486kph). **Range:** 620 miles (1000km). **Armament:** 2×0.5" (12.7mm) Breda-SAFAT machine guns.

Leaning Towards Europe

The problems facing Dowding's successor were very different from those he had encountered, and the demands made upon Fighter Command over coming months would vary with the ebb and flow of the war. Air Vice-Marshal Sholto Douglas arrived after the Battle of Britain was won and invasion no longer hung in the air like a permanent threat; but the Luftwaffe's challenge had not evaporated. Britain still stood alone against the Nazi madman; until he and his evil were subdued, the RAF's fighters would be in action.

The new AOC-in-C had been in favour of Bader's 'wings' but there was no opportunity yet to try them out. Just as Dowding had found, there was little Sholto Douglas could do against the night raiders until a means was found of 'seeing' them in the dark. A high-level committee was set up to consider the problem, and, until the AI sets fitted in Blenheim aircraft could be relied upon and their operators began to achieve more success, one interim solution put forward was to establish a number of specialist night-fighter squadrons.

The Hurricane and Defiant pilots who found themselves detailed for night-fighter duties were deeply sceptical at first. Radar information was imprecise; pilots needed to make visual contact with the enemy. Not only did they risk flying into hills or obstacles themselves, but the AA batteries could not distinguish friend from foe in the darkness. However, the specialist aircrew began to learn the best way to use whatever light was available, to close their eyes to searchlights but focus on shadows and silhouettes, to recognize the enemy in the reflected light of his own handiwork. It was still difficult and dangerous, but early in the new year they would start to see results.

One problem Sholto Douglas did not face was shortage of aircraft; production was rising and wastage was far less. Pilot strength was back to pre-Battle levels too; by the spring of 1941 there would be 1240 fighters and 1702 pilots to fly them. He could afford to start thinking aggressively, and developed a policy of 'leaning forward into France', as he put it.

Taking a leaf out of the Luftwaffe's book he launched fast, low sweeps across the Channel, a pair of fighters together, to strafe any suitable target they found: an enemy airbase, gun emplacement or radio transmitter. At first merely pinpricks, the irritant value of these raids would increase over coming months until finally whole wings could be deployed. Huge fighter escorts led the bombers towards their targets, luring the Bf.109s into action just as the Messerschmitts had once provoked them. It was the RAF fighters who pulled the puppet strings now, and the Germans who were forced to respond, to jump when the strings were jerked.

Bomber Command, of course, was likewise taking the war into Europe, and when the new four-engined Stirling arrived — followed in due course by the Halifax and the superb Avro Lancaster — the RAF offensive began to take shape.

At first Bomber Command struck against military targets in Germany and Italy but the accuracy and effectiveness of these attacks was over-optimistic. Intelligence was poor and no telling damage was inflicted. During 1940 and for the greater part of 1941, Germany had no cohesive defence against bombing attacks. No consideration had been given to the possibility of the British striking back at the Third Reich with any determination. When the British introduced these larger and more advanced aircraft, however, coupled with increasingly accurate navigational techniques, the Luftwaffe was forced to divert a large proportion of its effort into the defence of the Reich.

Taking over as Air Officer Commanding-in-Chief Bomber Command in February 1942, Air Marshal Arthur Harris saw the need to make a dramatic show of force. Harris firmly believed that Germany could be defeated by air power alone and began to escalate the scale of attacks against Germany. Kiel was bombed on three consecutive nights — 25, 26 and 27 February. Essen and Duisburg were bombed on 9 March and Lübeck was destroyed by fire on 28 March. Hitler ordered reprisal attacks in the form of raids on English historic towns featured in the Baedeker Tourist Guide. Exeter, Bath, Norwich, York and Camterbury were attacked between 23 April and 30 June 1942. On the four nights, 23 to 26 April, the RAF destroyed Rostock. On Saturday 30 May, Harris launched the first 1000-bomber raid — against Cologne. 18,472 houses and buildings were destroyed and 368 industrial plants hit; 486 people were killed, over 500 injured and 60,000 made homeless. By the end of the war every city and town in Germany had felt the weight of Bomber Command, but the cost was high with over 8000 aircraft and 47,000 aircrew lost.

Retribution

On 22 June 1941, Hitler's armies invaded the Soviet Union. Operation Barbarossa had begun, the operation he had started planning back in November 1940 when he was forced to abandon his invasion of Britain. Barbarossa was the largest military operation in history, involving seventy-nine German divisions. But it was doomed to failure. Hitler had badly underestimated both the Red Army's fighting abilities and the Russian people's resilience. He was forced to pull military and Luftwaffe units out of the Western Front to bolster his efforts in the east. Six months later his armies were still bogged down on the Eastern Front, when a catastrophic mistake by his other ally, Japan, brought the United States into the war on Britain's side.

Quick to accept the challenge of Pearl Harbour, the Americans had the colossal strength required to fight the war both in the Pacific and in Europe. Men and equipment were poured into Britain until in June 1944 they spilled across the Channel into France, eventually to link up with those who had returned to Europe via the Mediterranean. And the American heavy-bomber pilots in their B.17 Flying Fortresses and B.24 Liberators used Britain as a springboard into the occupied countries and Germany.

There remained a long and painful haul to ultimate victory in Europe. The US air forces had to learn many lessons that the RAF had already learnt the hard way; the newcomers sometimes rejected the advice offered by their British counterparts. Thus the Flying Fortresses and Liberators, operating in daylight, were at first wiped out of the sky by the Luftwaffe and the ground defences, despite their own formidable armament. Their losses were cut only when long-range fighters like the P.51 Mustang and P.47 Thunderbolt were fitted with drop tanks to carry extra fuel, and introduced as escorts; the American fighters, in turn, had to learn new tactics before they could overcome the skilled and practised Luftwaffe.

Slowly, agonizingly slowly, day by day, with many a setback, the enemy was pushed back behind his own borders. The Nazi tide was ebbing. Hitler's eleventh-hour deployment of his wonder-weapons, the V-1 'doodlebugs' and V-2 rockets, failed to bring the British to their knees. He raged in vain; the German High Command cast around in desperation, but found no way to appease him. Cornered in his bunker in Berlin, on 30 April 1945, the Führer shot himself. His Reichsmarschall surrendered and was held for trial; but on 15 October 1946 Göring too committed suicide.

Five years of total war had cost the lives of over sixteen million servicemen and women and thirty-seven million civilians from all over the world. Great Britain and the Commonwealth lost 373,372 service personnel with half a million wounded; over 93,000 civilians were killed. Approximately three and a half million German service personnel were killed and around 78,000 civilians. 292,131 American troops were killed and 6000 civilians. Estimates of the total Russian dead are in the region of fourteen million.

When Europe's stunned survivors wakened from the deadly nightmare and looked around them, there were some who asked what it was all for. Such terrible loss of life. Such destruction of beautiful medieval cities. Such waste. But when the hidden horrors of Belsen and Auschwitz were brought to light, the extermination camps, the sadistic experiments, the Jewish holocaust, then the world knew why Hitler had had to be stopped. Britain gave renewed thanks for the young men who had fought back the menace in the summer of 1940. As Churchill had promised, the nation would indeed marvel at their daring and their achievements, and say: 'This was their finest hour.'

'The gratitude of every home in our Island, in our Empire, and indeed throughout the world, except in the abodes of the guilty, goes out to the British airmen, who, undaunted by odds, unwearied in their constant challenge and mortal danger, are turning the tide of world war by their prowess and devotion. Never in the field of human conflict was so much owed by so many to so few.'

WINSTON CHURCHILL, 20 AUGUST 1940

Glossary

A

Aerial: Antenna on aircraft for RT communication.

Aerofoil: Shape of section of aircraft's wing. A thick section gives greater rate of climb and weight-carrying, a thin section higher speed.

AFB: Auxiliary Fire Brigade.

AI: Airborne Interception.

Aileron: Hinged surfaces on the outer part of the wings of an aircraft which control the rolling axis.

Air brakes: Panels or flaps pushed into airflow to slow an aircraft, particularly dive-bombers in a dive for more accurate bombing.

Airscrew: RAF jargon word for propeller.

ARP: Air Raid Patrol. Volunteer organization responsible for air-raid regulations, including fire watching, bomb marking, rescue and black-out regulations.

ASI: Air speed indicator.

ASR: Air–Sea Rescue. Boat and sea-plane rescue systems to recover aircrew fallen into the sea. Better organized by Germany.

ATA: Air Transport Auxiliary. A uniformed volunteer civilian organization of male and female pilots who ferried every sort of aircraft from manufacturers, MUs and CRUs to units.

Auxiliary Air Force: A peacetime training scheme set up in 1936 by which interested people could learn to fly or learn air force trades in their spare time. Members were absorbed into the RAF on the outbreak of WWII.

B

Battle-dress: Workaday uniform.

Beauty-chorus: Slang name for the WAAF plotters in the operations rooms.

Blood-wagon: RAF slang for ambulance.

Boiler-suit: One-piece overall.

Bomb disposal: The dangerous task of disarming unexploded or delayed-action bombs, usually carried out by skilled army officers and NCOs.

Bounce: Slang for surprising an enemy from above, often out of the sun.

Break: Order over RT to scatter or turn violently to avoid attack.

Brolly: Slang for parachute.

Bucket seat: Hollow seat, usually in a fighter, designed to hold pilot's parachute as a cushion.

Bumph: RAF slang for paperwork.

C

Call-sign: The codename used by controllers to identify each squadron over the RT. The call-sign was a two-syllable word, such as LUTON, LORAG and SILVA.

Carrots: Said to be good for the eyes, but really a myth put out to hide the use of AI radar. Still believed today, raw carrots are actually harmful to night sight if eaten to excess.

Caterpillar Club: A club of airmen who had survived an otherwise fatal crash by baling out and using a parachute. Members are entitled to wear a badge showing a silkworm.

Chain Home: CH — codename for RAF radar stations for long-range detection, up to 100 miles in good conditions.

Chain Home Low: CHL — code-name for low-level radar chain, with range of 30–40 miles but which could spot low-level raids.

Checks: A pilot had (and has) a number of checks to carry out for various parts of a flight, to ensure that the aircraft was correctly regulated. There are starting, pre-taxi, pre-take-off and landing checks. Most have a mnemonic to remind one of the procedure. For example, before starting a Spitfire, the pilot carries out BTFCPPUR — Brakes (on), Trim (neutral), Flaps (up), Contacts (ignition — off), Pressure (for undercarriage/flaps), Petrol (on), Undercarriage (lever down) and Radiator (open).

Cheesed-off: RAF slang — fed up.

Contrail: Condensation trail, now common, but novel at the time of the Battle, formed by the water-vapour in engine exhaust condensing as a line to mark the passage of an aircraft.

Controller: An officer, usually at Group or Sector operations rooms, who oversees the operations table and tells fighters where to go to intercept a raid.

Controller's Code: Words used between the controller and squadron commander to direct fighters to intercept enemy forces:

  Angels: Height, expressed in 1000s of feet — 'Angels 15' = 15,000ft.

  Bandit: Enemy aircraft.

  Bogy: Unidentified plot.

  Buster: 'Flat out', through the 'gate'.

  Liner: Cruising speed.

  Orbit: Circle and wait.

  Scramble: Take off.

  Tally-ho!: Squadron commander to controller, 'enemy sighted'.

  Trade: Enemy aircraft; customers.

  Pancake: Land at base.

  Vector: Course, as in 'Vector 90', 'steer course due East'.

Crash-waggon: RAF slang for Station Fire Engine.

CRO: Civilian Repair Organisation, set up in 1939 under Lord Nuffield, to ease aircraft supply by repairing damaged aircraft.

Crosswind landing: Aircraft at this time landed into the wind, indicated by a wooden 'T' or 'windsock'. If, however, a hard runway had to be used, a special 'crosswind landing' technique was employed. This entailed holding windward stick and rudder on until the wheels touched the ground. Unless skilled, this often ended in a ground-loop.

D

Deflection: Firing ahead of a target to allow for the forward movement of an enemy aircraft.

de-Wilde: A form of machine-gun ammunition which flashed when it hit an enemy aircraft, and therefore very useful for checking aim.

Dive-brakes: Surfaces extended from wings or fuselage used to slow an aircraft when diving to allow more accurate dive-bombing.

Dope: A highly inflammable acetate-based cellulose paint used to tighten and colour canvas on fabric-covered aircraft.

Douhet: Italian General who wrote a prophetic book, published in 1930, describing how bombers would win wars. Highly influential to official thinking, though proved wrong during much of WWII.

Dunking: To end in water by ditching or parachute.

Dural: A hard, strong, malleable but light alloy of aluminium used for aircraft construction.

E

Echelon: A formation in which each aircraft is stepped back outside the other to one side (either to Port or Starboard) of the leader.

Emil: Luftwaffe nickname for the Bf.109E fighter.

ENSA: Entertainers' National Service Association, an organization of show-people who put on entertainments for servicemen. To the sufferers, it became known as 'Every Night Something Awful'.

Establishment: The equipment, officers, NCOs and airmen required by a unit, whatever it is, necessary to carry out its function.

Experten: Luftwaffe term for Ace.

F

Fillet: Metal shape to fill joins between the fuselage and wing/tail surfaces.

Filter room: Part of the Fighter Command Operations Room, where friendly and mistaken reports are identified and removed from the Ops Room Table.

Flamer: RAF slang — aircraft shot down in flames.

Flare-out: To ease the stick back at the end of a landing approach to level an aircraft on to the ground. Nowadays known as 'round-out'.

Float plane: Aircraft with floats to land on water.

'Flying Pencil': Press and RAF slang for the Do.17/215.

Form 700: Official service log for each aircraft, signed by the plot to say it is in good condition.

Formations: Grouping of aircraft. The RAF, during the Battle, kept a pattern of vics of 3 and built on these to form an operating squadron. The Luftwaffe, on the basis of Spanish Civil War experience, used a *Rotte* of 2, doubled to a *Schwarm* of 4 aircraft, three *Schwärme* making a Staffel.

Freyer: German shore-to-ship radar. An example was set up on the cliffs above Cap Gris Nez.

G

Gate: The wire restriction on the throttle lever which, when broken, gave extra emergency power but which, when used, overstressed the engine so that it shortened its service life. This, during the Battle, became an everyday occurrence.

GCI: Ground-Controlled Interception. The system of control using Radar and Observer Corps reports, plotted on an operations table, to tell fighters where to intercept an enemy raid.

Gen: RAF slang for information, as in 'What's the gen?'.

Geodetic: A form of metal airframe construction based on diagonals, designed by Barnes Wallis for Vickers aircraft.

Glycol: Ethylene/glycerine liquid with high boiling temperature, used as an engine coolant for in-line engines.

Gong: RAF slang for medal.

Graf Zeppelin: Giant German rigid airship, used in 1939 to test the British radar emissions. Though plotted all the way up the east coast, and at one time over the Humber estuary, it failed to detect any electronic pulses, and reported that Britain did not have radar.

Ground-loop: A vicious swing on landing or take-off, where the aircraft turns right round, often losing the undercarriage and damaging wings and propeller.

Gruppe: German administrative unit, a subdivision of a Luftflotte roughly equivalent to an RAF Wing, although it might contain a mixture of fighters and bombers.

Guinea-Pig Club: A club formed of aircrew who had burns repaired at Sir Hector McIndoe's plastic surgery unit at East Grinstead.

Gunsight: During the Battle, both sides used a reflector gunsight which projected a range and sighting marker on a clear glass screen. Graticules indicated range and deflection for particular types of enemy aircraft.

H

HDV: Home Defence Volunteers, later to become known as the Home Guard and now known as 'Dad's Army'.

HE: High Explosive in bombs, mines or shells.

Hedge-hopping: Slang for flying very low, often necessary to escape pursuing aircraft but often done illegally for high spirits.

Hurrie: RAF slang for Hurricane.

I

IFF: Radio transponder which enhances a radar signal and re-transmits it to enhance a blip on the screen to identify friendly aircraft.

Irvin: Fur-lined leather flying jacket.

J

Jabo: *Jagdgeschwader*, German for fighter-bomber.

Jam: Of guns, to fail to fire, due to rounds or mechanisms seizing up. The early cannons were very prone to jamming, due to being fitted on their sides in Spitfires.

K

Knickebein: (Bent leg) — Code-name for a German Lorentz Beam blind bombing aid, used in late 1940 but jammed by the British.

L

Lorentz Beam: A navigational aid, using the overlapping of two narrow radio beams. Adapted for Knickebein and X-Geraint blind bombing aids.

M

Magneto: Ignition coil to produce high DC current for the spark plugs. Often got damp, so after starting they were checked by running up the engine, turning off each magneto switch and seeing how engine revs dropped.

Medals: Both the RAF and Luftwaffe aircrews were awarded medals which, despite disparagement (the RAF called them 'gongs'), were prized:

RAF: The Victoria Cross (VC), for an act of outstanding bravery — only one was won by Fighter Command during the Battle. The Distinguished Service Order (DSO), awarded to commanders for inspiration, bravery and example. The Distinguished Flying Cross (DFC), for acts of bravery or a good score. Distinguished Flying Medal (DFM) and Air Force Medal to other ranks. Winning any medal twice won a bar, a small metal tag worn on the medal ribbon on uniform.

Luftwaffe: The Blue Max (pour le mérite) for high scores or inspired leadership. The Iron Cross — 1st, 2nd or 3rd Class — for high scores or acts of bravery, with oak leaves to upgrade each level. The RAF wore medals only on special parades or functions, the Luftwaffe could wear medals on everyday uniforms.

Met. Reports: The daily weather report. Britain had the advantage, produced by a westerly prevailing wind, of knowing what the weather was likely to be ahead of the Luftwaffe.

Mess: Eating canteen/restaurant. Free for airmen, paid for by NCOs and Officers by wage deduction.

Mods: Slang for modifications, the changes necessary to bring an aircraft up to current specification.

Monocular or Monocoque: A method of aircraft building in which the skin of the structure carries the stress and thus needs less framework.

MUs: A series of RAF repair and modification workshops to handle work more complicated than could be managed at squadron level.

N

NAAFI: Navy, Army and Air Force Institute — a voluntary organization set up to run canteens and vans serving meals, tea and wads.

O

Observer Corps: A voluntary organization which spotted, identified and gave details of height and course of aircraft movements inland of the radar screen during the Battle.

P

Petter: Petrol bowser with a motorized pump.

'Piece of Cake': RAF slang meaning 'easy'.

Pipsqueak: A device in fighters to send a short RT signal every minute to enable controllers to obtain a fix for plotting their position.

Plot: A marker on the plotting table.

Plotting Table: The gridded map table on which plots were recorded in the Ops Room.

'Prang': RAF slang for crash.

R

R&R: Refuelling and rearming.

RDF: Radio Direction Finding, later called radar.

Range: The distance an aircraft can fly on a tank of fuel. Although measured as a mean distance, it also depends on the return distance to a base (or a diversionary airfield) and the power needed for combat.

Rotte: Pair of German aircraft.

S

Score: The 'kills' credited to a fighter pilot.

Sealion: The codename for the German plans to invade Britain.

Self-sealing: Of fuel tanks. A soft rubber lining which filled bullet holes and stopped fuel leaking out, and reduced the chance of a petrol fire. Not fitted during the Battle due to a misunderstanding in the 1930s, when tests on 'self-sealing' were confused with 'crash-proof' tanks, which had to be dropped from a great height onto concrete — the tanks broke, not surprisingly. 'Self-sealing' worked. This error cost a lot of lives and dire injuries during the Battle.

Shadow Factory: A parallel manufacturing unit, set up out of the way to avoid damage or disruption due to enemy raids.

Sortie: One operational flight from take-off to landing.

Spit: RAF slang for Spitfire.

Squadron: An RAF flying formation of 12 aircraft. A squadron was a self-organized unit, and could be switched from Sector or Group without losing its identity, squadron number or identifying letters (painted on the aircraft). Like a Staffel, a Squadron's ideal peacetime establishment comprised 18 aircraft and 22 pilots plus reserves — a condition seldom met during the Battle.

Staffel: A Luftwaffe flying formation of 12 aircraft, the equivalent of an RAF Squadron. Numbered as aircraft within the Staffel and within the Gruppe.

Stuffed Cloud: RAF slang for a cloud which contains a hill or mountain.

T

Taps: RAF slang for controls.

Three-pointer: A well-judged landing where the flare-out was held so that all three landing wheels touched the ground at the same time.

Tit: Gun-firing button, usually on control column.

Track: The width of the main-wheels of an aircraft's undercarriage.

Trolley-ac: Accumulator trolley — a hand-pulled, heavy-duty battery on wheels, charged by a small engine, which could be plugged into an aircraft to provide the power for starting without draining its own batteries.

Trumpets of Jericho: German name for sirens fitted to Ju.87 which made a terrifying scream during dive-bombing.

Turning Circle: The ability to turn inside an enemy's aircraft. The Spitfires were best, then Bf.109s, then Hurricanes, but this depended on height and speed.

Twitch: RAF slang for fear, coming from a feeling that the corners of one's eyes or mouth were constantly twitching.

2/5: Ground engine test, which entailed running up engine to full power while ground crew squatted on the tail to stop the aircraft nosing over or climbing over its chocks. One WAAF survived a circuit after failing to let go before take-off.

V

Vic: 3 RAF aircraft in close triangular formation.

W

WAAF: Women's Auxiliary Air Force, later called the WRAF. Women worked in a number of trades in the RAF, including admin., driving, and engineering.

Wad: A bun, usually dry.

Wallop: Slang for beer.

Wheeler: The opposite of a three-point landing, where an aircraft touches down on the two main-wheels first.

Wing: A formation of two or more Squadrons (up to five) under single command.

X

X-Geraint: German radio-beam bombing aid, similar to Knickebein.

Bibliography

AIR MINISTRY; *The Battle of Britain*; London; 1941.
AIR MINISTRY; *Pilot's Notes: Spitfire IIA and IIB Aeroplanes. Merlin XII Engine*; London?; 1940?
BICKERS, Peter Townsend; *Ginger Lacey — Fighter Pilot*; London; 1962.
BISHOP, Edward; *The Battle of Britain*; London; 1960
BRAMSON, Alan & BIRCH, Neville; *The Tiger Moth Story*; London; 1964.
BRICKHILL, Paul; *Reach for the Sky*; London; 1955.
CAIDIN, Martin; *Me 109*; London; 1969.
CAIN, Charles W. (Ed.); *Flypast* Vols 1, 3, 4, 8, 10; Windsor; 1972.
CHANTRAIN, J.P., *et al; Luftwaffe Uniforms*; London; 1989.
CHARLTON, L.E.O., *et al; The Air Defence of Britain*; Harmondsworth; 1938.
CHURCHILL, Winston S.; *The Second World War* Vols 1-4; London; 1948 & 1949.
CLOSTERMANN, Pierre; *Flames in the Sky*; London; 1952.
COLLIER, Richard; *Eagle Day*; London; 1981.
COOPER, Brian; *The Story of the Bomber 1914-1945*; London; 1974.
COOPER, Brian & BATCHELOR, John; *Fighter — A History of Fighter Aircraft*; London; 1973.
CULVER, Bruce & MURPHY, Bill; *Panzer Colours* Vols 1 & 2; London; 1976.
DEERE, , Alan C; *Nine Lives*; London; 1959.
DEIGHTON, Len; *Fighter*; London; 1977.
FEIST, Uwe; *The Fighting Me 109*; London; 1988.
FORRESTER, Larry; *Fly for your Life*; London; 1958.
FOXWORTH, Thomas G.; *The Speed Seekers*; London; 1989.
GALLAND, Adolf; *The First and The Last*; London; 1955.
GELB, Norman; *Scramble*; London; 1986.
GREEN, William; *Aircraft Augsburg Eagle — A Documentary History — Messerschmitt Bf 109*; London; 1980.

GUNSTON, Bill; *Aircraft of World War 2*; London; 1981.
GUNSTON, Bill (Ed.); *The Illustrated History of Fighters*; London; 1981.
HARBOROUGH PUBLISHING CO. LTD.; *Aircraft of the Fighting Powers* Vols 1-7; Leicester; 1940-1945.
HAY, Doddy; *War under the Red Ensign*; London; 1982.
HILLARY, Richard; *The Last Enemy*; London; 1942.
JOHNSON, J.E.; *Wing Leader*; London; 1956.
JONES, R.V.; *Most Secret War*; London; 1978.
KENT AVIATION HISTORICAL RESEARCH SOCIETY; *Kent Airfields in the Battle of Britain*; Rainham; 1981.
KNOKE, Heinz; *I Flew for Hitler*; London; 1953.
McKEE, Alexander; *The Coal-Scuttle Brigade*; London; 1957.
McKEE, Alexander; *Strike from the Sky*; London; 1960.
PRICE, Alfred; *The Spitfire Story*; London; 1982.
RAMSEY, Winston G. (Ed.); *The Battle of Britain*; London; 1989.
RAWNSLEY, C.F. & WRIGHT, Robert; *Night Fighter*; London; 1957.
RICHARDS, Denis; *Royal Airforce 1939-1945* Vol 1; London; 1953.
RICHARDSON, Anthony; *Wingless Victory*; London; 1953.
STONE, Norman; *Hitler*; London; 1980.
TOWNSEND, Peter; *Duel of Eagles*; London; 1970.
VADER, John; *Spitfire*; London; 1969.
WARD, Arthur; *A Nation Alone*; London; 1989.
WINCHESTER, Clarence (Ed.); *The Wonders of World Aviation* Vols 1-2; London; 1939
WOOD, Derek & DEMPSTER, Derek; *The Narrow Margin*; London; 1961.